T... H Y...

WRITING

ESSAYS & REPORTS

Paul Oliv...

Hodder & Stoughton

A MEMBER OF THE HODDER HEADLINE GROUP

Order : please contact Bookpoint Ltd, 39 Milton Park, Abingdon, Oxon OX14 4TD. Telephone: (44) 01235 400414, Fax: (44) 01235 400454. Lines are open from 9.00 – 6.00, Monday to Saturday, with a 24 hour message answering service. Email address: orders@bookpoint.co.uk

British Library Cataloguing in Publication Data
Oliver, Paul
Writing essays & reports. – (Teach yourself)
1.Report writing 2.Academic writing
I.Title
808'.066

ISBN 0 340 67010 X

First published 1996 Paul Oliver
Impression number 11 10 9 8 7 6 5 4
Year 2004 2003 2002 2001 2000 1999

Typeset by Transet Limited, Coventry, England.
Printed in Great Britain for Hodder & stoughton Educational, a division of Hodder Headline plc, 338 Euston Road, London NW1 3BH by Cox & Wyman Limited, Reading, Berks.

CONTENTS

FOREWORD

This book is intended to help you with your assignments at college and university. It covers all of the main kinds of assignments which you will come across. I have included general advice on writing styles, on ways of structuring your work, and strategies for helping you to use your time effectively. There are a lot of ways of using this book. You could read it cover to cover in one go, but I think it might be more useful to use it as a reference book, reading say the chapter on essay writing when you have an essay assignment coming up. You can keep checking up on different points as necessary.

Throughout the book there are boxes labelled 'Practical advice' which provide just that. You could also skim through the book, reminding yourself of these key points. They are intended for quick reference. The last three chapters provide advice on aspects which apply to all assignments: referencing, writing about theory, and checking and editing.

As a university tutor myself, I have also included a lot of information about the typical assessment process. I hope this will give you insights into how best to approach your work. There will never be any short cuts with assignments – they will always be hard work. However, careful planning and a sensible working strategy, can make the process less tiring and more enjoyable. I hope the advice in this book is of help to you.

So best wishes with all those assignments, and I hope you get good grades!

Paul Oliver

1

INTRODUCTION TO ACADEMIC WRITING

Academic writing is a skill, and like any other skill it is possible to learn it and to improve upon it. Assignments and essays are normally written in a particular style of language which is different to that used in other literary forms such as fiction or journalism. The academic style of writing does not come easily to all of us because it is unlike the normal form of language which we employ in conversation and everyday use. For one thing, academic writing is rather unemotional and impartial, and avoids attempts to express feelings. With practice, however, this style is not difficult to use and can be a precise form of communication.

In the sense that academic writing is used to summarise and convey ideas precisely, it has much in common with the styles of language used in business communication and in legal discussion. However, academic writing serves another important function and that is *analysis*. It helps us to break down complex ideas and arguments into their constituent parts and to examine each issue in detail. The related function of academic writing is in the *evaluation of evidence*. In this sense, evidence may be experimental data from a physics laboratory or an account of someone's life in an autobiography. In such cases, the evidence is typically discussed and weighed carefully in order to establish whether it can be relied upon, and then perhaps connections are made with other related evidence. The style of the writing is typically cautious and objective, taking care not to jump to hasty conclusions.

Writing skills can be learned

Perhaps the first step in learning to be proficient at writing essays and academic reports is to realise that a particular style of writing has to be acquired. This style of writing has its own rules and conventions, and these are different in many cases to those operating within other language styles. Generally, these conventions are clear and there is widespread agreement about the forms that academic writing can take. It is then, perfectly possible to learn these rules and to practise their application.

The above characteristics can be illustrated by examining a short piece of academic writing. This is taken from a discussion of the procedures followed by a researcher who was approaching people on the street to complete questionnaires about their favourite television programmes.

> The researcher collected the data by standing outside the town market from nine o'clock onwards on a Monday morning. He stopped men and women alternately, asking them if they would complete a brief questionnaire about their favourite television programmes. Before twelve noon, a total of twenty-two people had agreed to participate. The sample consisted of fourteen women and eight men.
>
> One of the advantages of this type of data collection is that it is convenient for the researcher. Potential respondents are literally walking past. However, those individuals who complete questionnaires may well be a very diverse group of people. They may have nothing in common other than that they have complied with a request to provide their opinions on television programmes. It is unclear, for example, whether individuals of a particular age group were selected; nor is evidence available concerning the number of people who refused to cooperate with the researcher.

In this extract there is a discussion about the way in which the research was carried out. However, the writer does not seem to give a personal opinion about the method used, nor to adopt a particular value position. Instead, a rather balanced view is taken. An advantage of the method is first noted, followed by one or two more critical comments. This attempt at being balanced and objective is one of the characteristics of good academic writing.

Another feature of the extract is that it does not take things for granted, but looks below the surface of what at first sight might seem reasonable and obvious. For example, it might seem sensible to stop people at random on the street, so that the researcher would get a balanced cross-section of people. On the other hand, as the writer points out, if those people are sigificantly different from each other, they may not be representative of any larger group of individuals. It may then be difficult to draw any firm conclusions from the questionnaires. This tendency to examine ideas carefully, and to dissect the underlying arguments is a key feature of academic writing.

Besides demonstrating analytical skills, the writer is also involved in the evaluation of evidence. Most academic writing involves trying to form soundly-based judgements about existing evidence. In many ways the process is similar to that of the detective confronted with small pieces of evidence, and trying to build up an accurate picture of the events leading up to a crime. In the last sentence of the extract, for example, the writer points out that it is likely that some people did not wish to complete a questionnaire, and that we are not told the number of such individuals. This could be important, because if a large number of people refused to take part, it might indicate that the interviewer was not using a good technique to approach people.

PRACTICAL ADVICE

When you are in conversation, reading a newspaper, or watching television, ask yourself whether you are being given all of the relevant information about a situation.

Has the writer or speaker already made up his or her mind about the issue, or is he or she still open-minded?

Are you being presented with a biased picture of an issue?

By thinking in this way, you will develop your *critical* abilities. This does not mean that you will criticise things, but that you will think more deeply and analytically about issues.

Structuring your ideas

Academic writing is generally much more structured than other types of writing. In forms of creative writing such as poems or novels, there is no particular structure to which the writer must adhere. In fact, it is sometimes a virtue to write in an unusual style. Academic writing is much more formalised however, and it is important to adjust to that formality.

Different types of writing have different purposes, and each has its own traditional structure. This book discusses a number of different structures within which students are asked to work. The essay has a different structure from that of the portfolio, which again is different from the research report. Although the structures of these different forms of academic writing are different, the *style* of writing employed is broadly the same. That is, it is characterised by an attempt at objectivity, at analysis, and at an evaluation of evidence.

There are good reasons for ensuring that academic writing is well structured. In a novel such as a crime thriller, the writer may start by describing the crime, and then develop the events which led up to that crime. On the other hand, the writer may deal with events in chronological order. It all depends upon the nature of the characters and plot, and the inclinations of the author. In academic writing however, the order of events is extremely important. A research report would seem strange if the writer described the analysis of results and the conclusion, before stating the data or evidence which had been gathered. If this were the case, then the reader would be unable to judge whether the results could reasonably be derived from the data. Academic writing is concerned with the logical analysis of evidence, and the writing must proceed in a series of logical stages.

In an essay or tutorial paper the student should be trying to develop a particular argument and in so doing to convince the reader of the truth of that argument. The most effective way to achieve this is to present the issues in a carefully ordered sequence so that the reader can easily appreciate the thought process of the writer. The order of the ideas should be so clear and transparent that the reader has no difficulty at all in following the argument. If the reader has to keep going back through the argument, and rereading in order to understand it, then there is probably something wrong with the structure of the writing.

A fairly close analogy is when someone asks for directions in a strange town. If the directions are clear and in the correct order, then the person will easily reach his or her destination. Good academic writing should set down the ideas clearly and in the correct order, so that the reader is led to the conclusion without getting lost on the way.

PRACTICAL ADVICE

A newspaper editorial is in many ways a kind of short essay. Within the space of five or six short paragraphs, the editor develops an argument about a topical issue and suggests a particular conclusion to the reader.

Read the editorial from a 'quality' newspaper and note down in a few words, the key point of each paragraph. You will then have a summary of the argument as presented by the editor, and the sequence of ideas leading to the conclusion.

You will often find in your own writing that it is helpful to carry out this process in reverse. That is to decide on the sequence of ideas in your argument, and then to write a paragraph or two around each idea.

Choosing an appropriate writing style

The traditional form of academic writing is to employ impersonal verbs in the third person singular. For example, instead of writing:

> I carried out an experiment to investigate the effect of light on plant growth.

it would be more conventional to say:

> An experiment was carried out to investigate the effect of light on plant growth.

The main reason for writing impersonally is that it is perhaps easier to be impartial and objective. There is less of a tendency to relate what we are saying to our own feelings or experiences. This is particularly important in any kind of scientific enquiry where in an ideal situation, it should not matter who is conducting the investigation. The focus is upon the data and upon the analysis of that data. Ideally, if a scientific investigation is completely reliable, then two scientists working independently should obtain the same results. That this should actually happen is, for all kinds of reasons, improbable, but nevertheless the focus of scientific enquiry is always upon the research and not upon the researcher. (For the sake of consistency, we are going to follow the convention that 'data' is singular.)

This approach is found particularly in the so-called natural sciences, such as chemistry and physics, but has also spread into most other subject areas. While this style of writing has the undoubted advantage that it encourages impartiality and discourages too much personal involvement in what is written, it has at least one potential disadvantage. It does tend to produce prose which can be somewhat flat and uninteresting. Perhaps for this and other reasons, there has been a recent tendency in some subject areas to encourage the limited use of the first person singular. This is particularly true of, say, the social sciences, where sometimes the interaction between individuals and the situations in which they find themselves is significant. Examples of the use of the first person singular are as follows:

> I made enquiries at my workplace for colleagues who would be willing to be interviewed, but most people were cautious about taking part in a research project.
>
> I started to collect data on football crowd behaviour and attended football matches every Saturday. I found myself tending to be drawn into the culture of the football supporter.

This style of writing tends to be used in specific situations, and it is probably best for students to consult their tutors before using it. The impersonal style of writing remains the norm for the types of assignment discussed in this book. Some examples of its use are as follows:

> It was decided to employ questionnaires for this enquiry because of the need to collect information from a large number of people.
>
> It became evident that the liquid was evaporating more rapidly than in the first test.
>
> Although the painting had been subjected to considerable atmospheric pollution, it was felt that restoration was still a distinct possibility.

Besides writing in an impersonal way, another important feature of an academic writing style is the attempt to show caution and restraint in describing events, making predictions and drawing conclusions. For example, instead of saying:

> The European war was caused by the blockade of the Atlantic ports.

it would be preferable to suggest that:

> The blockade of the Atlantic ports was a major contributory factor to the start of the European war.

The reason for this caution is that it is difficult to obtain absolutely accurate explanations for events. Even events taking place in a scientific laboratory are subject to the same kinds of uncertainties. When taking readings with measuring instruments, for example, a physicist must be aware of the limitations to the accuracy of the data. This is evidently so in the humanities subjects as well. Historical explanation depends on the nature of the data available, and such data is rarely as satisfactory or complete as historians would wish. Caution must, therefore, be exercised in coming to conclusions, and this caution should be reflected in the style of language adopted.

For example, in an essay discussing say an imaginary situation where a conspirator plotted the downfall of a head of state, the extant evidence may suggest that the conspirator acted out of altruistic reasons for the welfare of the country. This conclusion might derive from evidence such as contemporary political documents, newspaper accounts and personal diaries. However, it is difficult enough to determine the motives of a living individual, let alone a historical figure. It is, therefore, important to reflect this uncertainty in an essay or research report. The kinds of phrases which might be used are as follows:

> The evidence *seems to suggest* that the conspirator was not acting out of envy or personal hatred.
>
> The political documents which we have available certainly *incline us to suppose* that altruism may have been behind the conspirator's actions.
>
> That the conspirator acted out of personal dislike for the head of state, does not *seem* to have been the opinion of those journalists writing at the time.

> In the speeches made prior to the coup d'état, the conspirator certainly *gives the impression* of being motivated by altruism for the people of the country.

In the above examples, the words or phrases which qualify the certainty of the sentence are in italics. These words leave room for alternative explanations. After all, in any area of academic investigation, new data can emerge, long-lost documents may be found, or unanticipated results emerge from an experiment. By using qualifying words such as these, it is possible to express caution and to leave open the possibility of alternative explanation.

Writing to a format

The written word can be constructed into many different forms, including, for example, the poem, the play, the novel and the business marketing report. Over the years, certain written formats have become regarded as most suitable within an academic context, and are, therefore, set as assignments by teachers and lecturers, and also find their way into examinations in one form or another. The structure of these formats has developed over time, and indeed is still evolving, but there is close agreement within education of what constitutes a good essay or a good research report. Such is the closeness of international communication between educationalists now, that there would be little difference in opinion between what was regarded as a good assignment in say Australia, or the United States or Europe. The ground rules, as it were, are fairly closely defined. The following is a brief summary of the characteristics of the main formats discussed in subsequent chapters.

The essay

As a literary form, the essay has a long history. In the sixteenth century, Francis Bacon was a leading exponent, and in more recent times both Aldous Huxley and Virginia Woolf have written influential essays. The essay sets out to explore a specific issue or closely defined problem. It is generally not sufficiently long to accommodate a lot of illustrative material, and usually relies upon a careful analysis of summaries of data, or of 'facts' which are given temporary credence within the context of the essay.

The essay usually starts with a clear introduction which summarises the issue to be discussed and explains the limits or parameters of the discussion. It may be necessary to define some technical terms in the introduction in order to avoid later confusion. There then follows a detailed evaluation of the issue, which traditionally presents the different sides of the argument. This is sometimes known as examining an issue from a number of different perspectives. It is possible to write an essay from only one perspective, but in that case it is crucially important to explain this in the introduction so that the reader is aware of the viewpoint from which the essay is written. The essay should end with a concise conclusion which draws together and contrasts the main points raised in the essay.

The essay is employed as a means of assessment in a wide range of subjects. In English and philosophy it is used to examine ability at constructing arguments and in verbal precision, while in subjects such as biology, psychology and history it is used in addition to test subject matter knowledge.

The portfolio

The portfolio has been traditionally associated with art and design courses, where students gather together a selection of their best creative work for assessment. The work has literally been placed in a large cardboard portfolio. In recent years, however, the idea of asking students to collect together a range of work or materials produced, and to submit these for assessment has been gaining popularity in education. It has been shown to be particularly relevant for mature students who are studying part-time. It is acknowledged that they may have acquired skills and knowledge in the workplace or elsewhere, which are relevant to an academic course. If this is the case, they are encouraged to gather together evidence of that knowledge into a portfolio and to submit it for assessment. The evidence may consist, for example, of documents they have produced or of statements by referees verifying that certain skills are possessed.

The impact of the portfolio has been felt particularly on work-related or vocational courses. The challenge for the student is to be aware of how to select the most appropriate artefacts to include in the portfolio, and then how to organise the material for inclusion. The portfolio is relatively new and still developing as a form of assessment. It is not limited to any particular subject areas, but is more likely to be found on programmes with a vocational orientation.

The seminar or tutorial paper

Unlike the essay which is clearly used throughout the school and college system, the seminar paper is much more characteristic of university studies. The seminar or tutorial is a meeting between student and tutor. The word 'seminar' tends to be used for a situation where a small group of students, perhaps five or six, meet their tutor for a discussion about a specific topic. The 'tutorial' on the other hand, is more normally a one-to-one meeting between student and tutor.

In both cases, a topic is agreed prior to the meeting, and in the case of the seminar, usually a single student agrees to prepare a discussion paper on the chosen subject. The same system operates with the tutorial. A copy of the discussion paper is circulated to the tutor and, in the case of the seminar, to other students, prior to the meeting. At the seminar, the student may be asked to read the paper in full, or perhaps more typically, to provide a brief oral summary of the contents. There then ensues a general discussion about the contents with the tutor using the paper as a vehicle to draw out the important teaching issues.

On some courses, seminar papers may actually be assessed and graded, but it is generally more usual for them to be used as a medium for teaching. They are important, however, as they provide the tutor with direct evidence of the progress of students, and of their ability to articulate their views.

The research report

During the last years of high school or early years of college or university, most students are asked at some time to carry out a short study which involves them in collecting and analysing information. This kind of assignment can have various names including a project, long study, investigation or research project. No doubt on some courses, other names are used as well. The main feature of such an assignment is that the student is asked to collect some data. This may involve using interviews or questionnaires, or conducting an experiment, or collecting documentary material. The data is then analysed and the student draws various conclusions. To term this a 'research project' does not seem unduly inaccurate, but it should be distinguished from a thesis or dissertation. These terms are reserved for the much longer pieces of work associated with research degrees such as the Master or Doctorate in Philosophy. Although the structure may be broadly the same, a much more detailed treatment of research methodology is required, and they are outside the scope of this book.

The word 'research' may create an impression of high-level work conducted exclusively in a university, but the term may reasonably be applied to any form of planned and systematic investigation. The normal procedure is that the student agrees the subject for the research with the tutor, and plans a strategy for collecting and analysing the data. Once the data has been collected, the research report can be written, providing a summary of the methods used and the way in which the conclusions were drawn.

If the work has involved collecting information from people, it is often important to preserve their anonymity by, for example, using fictional names in the final report. Such ethical issues are becoming increasingly important in research, and it is important to give them due consideration. Sometimes research reports can find wider circulation, for example by being published in one form or another, and this makes it even more important that the privacy of individuals is not infringed.

In Chapter 2 we can look at some general aspects of planning and organising these different forms of assignment, before examining each in more detail.

Summary

- Academic writing is a skill which you can learn and improve upon.
- When you are writing:
    - Try to be as objective and balanced as you can;
    - Try to analyse ideas in order to reveal underlying meanings;

  - Try to evaluate data or evidence as clearly and precisely as possible.
- Unless you have a special reason, write in the third person.
- Express yourself cautiously when making statements or drawing conclusions.

2
PLANNING AND ORGANISATION

The aims of the assignment

It is important when starting an assignment to have a clear idea of what is to be achieved. Aims are the ideas or issues which have been analysed by the end of an assignment and which had not been so discussed prior to starting the assignment. An example of an assignment could be *'to consider a major character in a novel, and to write an imaginary account of what happens to that character, once the novel is finished'*.

The aims for such an essay might be:

- To develop a series of plausible events which could be a possible continuation to the plot of the novel;
- To chart the behaviour of the character in response to these events.
- To ensure that the character behaves consistently with the personality developed in the main novel;
- To link the behaviour of the character to that of other individuals in the book.

These aims will condition the overall approach to the assignment. They are not the same as the plan for the essay. This would be much more precise, setting out almost paragraph by paragraph, the main topics to be covered. The aims, however, set the main parameters for the piece of work, and most importantly, provide a check at the end, that the main goals of the assignment have been accomplished.

In an essay it is not usual to enumerate aims at the beginning or in the introductory paragraphs. The aims remain implicit rather than explicit. One device is to describe briefly the scope of the essay in the introduction, and this may, in effect, allude to some of the aims. In research or project reports, however, it is normal to list the aims near the beginning of the report. Aims should be written in a clear and concise style, and should be in such a form that it is possible to know by the end of the project whether or not they have been achieved. As an example, consider an investigation in psychology to determine the number of random digits which can be memorised by samples of people of different ages. Some aims for such an investigation might be:

- To investigate the capacity of short-term memory to learn a sequence of random digits;
- To investigate any potential relationship between short-term memory and age;
- To investigate other variables which may have an effect upon short-term memory.

When the data has been collected and analysed, and the conclusion is being written, it is invaluable to be able to check back to the aims to see whether in broad terms, they have been achieved. If, in fact, it has not been possible to achieve one or more of the aims, then it is a good idea to explain the reason in the conclusion.

Advice from your tutor

As assignment is set by a tutor in order to assess the extent to which a student has understood part of a course. It is reasonable to expect a tutor to have covered the skills and knowledge necessary for a student, in principle, to complete and pass an assignment. However, it is obviously expected of students, that they will read round a subject, and study in excess of the material presented in lectures and tutorials. Indeed, the extent of this extra studying may well distinguish between an excellent and indifferent final result. It is important that students ask their tutors for help and advice with assignments, if any following situations seem to apply:

1 The student feels that a central concept or idea has not been adequately explained in a lecture or tutorial;
2 The required format or structure of the assignment has not been adequately specified. This may refer to, for example, the need or otherwise to consult primary source material; or the extent of the bibliography required;
3 The layout of the assignment has not been specified. This may refer to such issues as whether word processing is required, or whether double line-spacing is necessary.

Should one or more of these issues be unclear, then it is reasonable for the student to ask for a short tutorial, or perhaps some information on a handout, if this is available.

It is important to try to follow the tutor's advice. Most coursework assignments at either high school, college or university are assessed by the tutor who has taught the unit, and who has set the assignment. Such tutors should be familiar with the assessment procedures and regulations, and therefore in a position to give the most relevant advice.

Sometimes students ask their tutors if they can submit a draft of an assignment for comment, prior to it being formally assessed. Indeed, tutors will sometimes offer to do this as part of the tutorial advisory process. However, it is important that students do not expect the comments on a draft to be extremely detailed. Some tutors may correct grammatical and spelling errors for example, but more usually they would probably restrict themselves to more general comments on the content and the types of argument used. If the comments become too detailed, then there is a danger that the essay or project will seem to have been drafted by the tutor.

If a tutor is willing to comment on students' drafts, then perhaps the best approach is for students to ask for advice on general issues about which they may feel uncertain. These might include:

- the general layout of the essay or project
- the system of referencing used
- the recency of works cited in the bibliography
- the way in which theoretical issues have been incorporated into the assignment
- the way in which evidence has been analysed
- the way in which conclusions have been reached

> *PRACTICAL ADVICE*
>
> If your tutor is willing to provide feedback on an essay or project, then once your draft is complete, think carefully about the issues upon which you would like advice. Make a list of these and hand it to your tutor along with the assignment. This will help the tutor when reading the draft. During the follow-up tutorial, this list will provide a focus for discussion. Make notes on the main points emerging from the tutorial, and use these to help you revise the assignment.

The assignment within the total course

Before an examination, most students are familiar with their teachers' advice to 'answer all the questions' and 'divide up your time evenly between questions'. The second piece of advice is based upon the assumption that all questions carry the same number of marks. Time management is essential not only in examinations, but also for the duration of a programme of study.

On most programmes there are assignments of different length, and which, therefore, are weighted differently for assessment purposes. Today, many programmes are modularised, or taught as units or modules. (In the United States, such modules are themselves called 'courses'.) Modules can be of different length, and attract different numbers of credit points. It would seem illogical and perhaps foolish to spend the same amount of time on a twenty-credit module as on a ten-credit module, unless there were unusual reasons to make this necessary.

Most students, whether full-time or part-time, have a finite amount of time to devote to their studies. Effective time management is an important skill for students to acquire. It is easy, for example, to continue doing the background reading for an assignment, never feeling quite certain when sufficient information has been collected. Such uncertainty can sometimes hide an unacknowledged reluctance to actually start writing the assignment! With such an approach, it is easy for students to get behind with their assignments, and then find that they have to rush through the last few pieces of work in order to meet deadlines. The result is that time has been allocated disproportionately, and almost inevitably there will be unnecessarily lower grades for some assignments.

The information on the sequence of modules for a programme is usually contained in a syllabus or handbook available from the tutor, and this document also states the number of credits allocated to each module. Submission dates for assignments are usually also made available at the beginning of a programme. This information can form the basis for a realistic time-management schedule.

> *PRACTICAL ADVICE*
>
> You can use time-management skills to plan a study schedule. Either buy or make a wall chart for the academic year. Mark on it the submission dates for assignments and also note the number of credit points allocated to each piece of work.
>
> Then sit down and think carefully about the amount of time you can realistically set aside for study each week. By adding this information to your wall chart, you should have an easily accessible record of the time you will devote to each assignment, in proportion to its relative importance in terms of credit points.

Assessment and grading

It is worth making the distinction between 'assessment' and 'grading'. The assessment of a piece of work is the overall process by which a judgement is reached about the academic quality of an essay or project. The grading of an assignment, on the other hand, is the process of allocating either a number or a letter which enables the quality of one piece of work to be compared with that of another. The terms used are normally 'numerical grade' or 'literal grade' respectively. Sometimes assignments are not graded, but are simply defined as being a 'pass' or a 'fail'. Sometimes an assignment can be 'referred'. This means that it has not been good enough to pass, but nor has it been sufficiently poor for it to be failed outright. The assignment may be resubmitted and reassessed. If it is of sufficient standard, it will pass.

Another term which is associated with assessment is that of 'moderation'. This is the sometimes complicated process of comparing work from one school, college or university, with that from comparable institutions in other parts of the country. The procedure is designed to try to ensure that standards are broadly comparable across the country.

The syllabus or course document produced by the institution should specify those assignments which will be ungraded and those which will be graded. In addition, such a document should specify the modules or units which contribute towards the final grade for the programme of study. At university, for example, it is not usually the norm for first-year grades to count towards the final grade (or classification) for the degree. It may be that not all of the work in the final two years will contribute towards the classification. Not only do university regulations differ, but courses within the same university also differ in the systems they use. It is important for students to make themselves familiar with the systems within which they are operating.

Length

A tutor's instructions for an assignment usually specify a recommended length. This is normally expressed as a particular number of words, or as a range of words such as three thousand to four thousand words. It is usually assumed that the word length quoted excludes the bibliography or list of references at the end of the assignment, and also any appendices. In other words it refers to the main text of the essay or research report.

There are reasons why it is helpful, indeed important, to place a word limit on an assignment. If a group of students was preparing an essay for which there was no length restriction, some would write a fairly short essay, and others would write much longer essays of varying length. If the writing was of more or less the same quality, there would be a tendency for the longer essays to attract the higher grades, simply because the writers had given themselves more space in which to express ideas. They would inevitably be able to cover the subject more widely. In other words, during the assessment process, the tutor would not be comparing like with like.

Another important reason for having a word limit is that it imposes a discipline upon the writer. With an assignment of finite length, the student has inevitably to be selective in the issues discussed and in the depth of the treatment. This enforced selectivity encourages clarity of thought, and the development of succinct arguments.

The length of a piece of work rarely becomes an issue with examination essays or questions, as the time limit of exams has the same effect as a word limit. It is however, important with coursework, where there are no such time limits. When the length of an assignment is expressed in terms of a range of words, it is rarely advisable simply to aim to produce the minimum number of words. This may be acceptable, if the work is of a very high standard, but it would normally be more prudent to aim for a length at least halfway between the minimum and the maximum.

Students are frequently concerned whether they will be penalised if they exceed the maximum number of words. In the experience of the author this is rarely, if ever, the case, although practices no doubt vary. However, although students may only infrequently be penalised for additional word length, they should not expect to be advantaged because they have chosen to exceed the recommended length. The most sensible course of action is to follow instructions and adhere to the word lengths.

The calculation of word lengths need not cause numeracy problems. Most word processors incorporate a 'word count' facility which does all the hard work. If, however, this is not available, then all that is necessary is an approximation of the word length. This can be achieved by counting the words on a fairly typical line of text or taking the average of several, and multiplying by the number of lines on the page, and then by the number of pages. The resulting figure will be a good working approximation.

Perhaps the most difficult aspect of achieving the requisite word length, is that as the essay or project is being written, it is not always easy to know whether too much is being written on one section, and an insufficient number of words allocated to an important section later in the assignment. Apart from developing a kind of intuition through experience, the only safe way to resolve this problem, is to plan the assignment and then allocate a specific number of words to each proposed section. In a research report, for example, it is normal to include a section where the student reviews the previous research in that particular area. If it is felt that this section should be three times as long as the introduction, then approximate word lengths can be allocated to the sections.

PRACTICAL ADVICE

When you are planning an assignment such as a project, work out in advance the main sections for the finished piece of work, and allocate a certain number of words to each. Ensure that these total up to the required word limit for the assignment. The length of different sections is a matter of judgement. Your tutor will provide advice on this. Your plan may look like this:

Introduction	500 words
Aims of the project	300 words
Method of data collection	700 words
Summary of data	900 words
Analysis of data	400 words
Conclusion	400 words

The anticipated word lengths of sections are only approximations, but they do provide a useful guide when writing an assignment. It is sometimes difficult to look ahead to the completion of an essay or paper which is say, 6000 words long, but it is far easier to have a target of writing a 500-word introduction. This is a much more achievable goal. In this way, a long piece of work can be broken down into subsections which are easier to think about, and which are more reasonable targets for completion.

Forms of presentation

In an age of widespread computer availability, it is definitely desirable that coursework essays and reports be word processed. Quite apart from the professional appearance, the ease of making amendments is a major advantage. The only possible disadvantage of computers is the temptation to make excessive use of desktop publishing facilities. If a project contains an over-abundance of ornate fonts, decorative borders, and complex artwork, this may detract from the content. At the end of the day, an essay or other assignment should be judged on the academic content and not on the presentation skills.

Word processing introduces the potential for such variety of presentation, that it probably best to adhere to a few reasonable conventions of format. The following are fairly commonly accepted:

Double-spacing This is a normal convention on manuscripts. In the case of a tutor commenting on a draft, or carrying out the final assessment, it is possible to write comments between lines much more easily. This is also helpful, when students are revising an assignment prior to making changes on the disk.

Number the pages The title page is usually not numbered.

Wide left-hand margin This allows extra space if an assignment is to be bound on the left-hand side. Otherwise, it can be difficult to read the first word of each line.

Quotations should be highlighted This can be done by using italics and by indenting by one tab space from the left-hand margin. This is further discussed in Chapter 8.

For the initial assessment it is wise to submit an assignment in a temporary binding, in case any amendments are required. Transparent plastic covers are widely used. It is important to keep a copy. It is a good idea to keep a paper copy, and *always* have a backup copy of your disk, which should be kept well away from the working copy, preferably in another building. (Just stop and think what you would lose it there was a fire!)

The other golden rule is to save your work regularly – a power cut can be advastating if it loses you half an essay!

Many institutions and departments will have their own 'style manual' which specifies the way in which assignments should be submitted. If available, this should obviously be complied with, but the above points are a reasonable guide to presentation. Many tutors ask for a 'cover sheet' to accompany each assignment, and even if not required it is a good idea to use one. It provides the student with a useful record of the assignment details.

PRACTICAL ADVICE

When you submit an assignment, attach at the front a 'cover sheet' which summarises all of the essential information about yourself, the course and the particular assignment. Your tutor may issue you with a standard format for this, but if not, some or all of the following information could be included:

- name of the institution
- name of the department
- your name
- student reference number (if you have one)
- assignment (or module) number and name
- course or programme name
- the title of your essay or research report
- the name of your tutor
- the date of submission

If you keep photocopies of all of your assignment cover sheets, then you will have an accurate record of work completed and submitted.

Preparatory reading

This is an essential part of the work for any assignment. Perhaps the major purpose of preliminary reading is to review the subject matter knowledge for the assignment, in order to ensure that arguments are as soundly based as possible. Background reading for this purpose can include lecture notes, handout material, set books, the books on reading lists, and other text books identified by the student. The bibliographies in books are a useful and speedy way to survey the literature in a particular field.

In order to review content knowledge, text books are probably preferable to edited collections of papers by different academics. The text book is written with the specific purpose of elucidating material for students, and is likely to be easier to understand.

Background reading is also important in order to collect references with which to justify arguments in the essay or research paper. For this purpose, edited collections are useful. They frequently consist of short summaries of research by different authors, collected around a particular theme. There is, therefore, access to the work of a number of different academics within a single volume. Papers in academic journals are another useful source of references. Such papers can range from the fairly straightforward to the extremely technical. The abstract or synopsis, which is usually printed at the beginning immediately below the title, is a good guide to the content of the paper.

Many students are justifiably concerned that they should refer only to recently published work. However, it is not an infallible rule that one should refer only to works published within, say, the last five years. There are two important aspects of this issue.

In most subjects or disciplines, one can nearly always think of significant books or papers, which at the time had a major influence on that particular academic area. They may have represented epoch-making research which moved that discipline forwards into a new era, or perhaps they are works where a leading academic has presented a definitive summary of that discipline at a particular stage in its development. Such works may have been published some time ago, yet may still retain their importance in the development of the subject area. Books which are potentially within this category are quite easy to identify during a literature search, because they tend to occur with great regularity in the bibliographies of books within the discipline. If a student is not familiar with the author, then the importance or otherwise of the work can be confirmed by a tutor.

It is perfectly legitimate to quote works which fall into this category even if they have been published some years ago. There should, of course, be a range of contemporary sources to provide a counterbalance to these older, seminal works.

The other reason why one may sometimes quote from older books is that recency is of more pressing importance in some subjects than in others. In an essay on human genetics, for example, it would seem strange to refer only to books written before the 1950s and the discovery of DNA. In the natural sciences, recency of information is normally of paramount importance. On the other hand, in a subject such as philosophy, there is not the same sequential advance in empirical knowledge. The subject is more about the clarity of analysis, and the nature of the arguments employed. The writings of the ancient Greek philosophers still have a great deal of relevance today, and can be applied to contemporary contexts. It would not seem at all strange to quote the works of Plato in a philosophy essay.

Modern indices and databases, many nowadays on CD-ROM, have made it far quicker and easier to access references in a particular subject area. However, there is frequently a problem of locating references on the particular narrow topic of a project or research report. The nature of research, even within a short study, necessitates a fairly focused and narrow topic for investigation. It is sometimes necessary to be satisfied with references to related topics, rather than to the narrow subject under investigation. An example will illustrate the difficulty.

Suppose that a project is being written on the subject of '*The settlement of European migrants in New York during the nineteenth century*'. On commencing a literature search, the first thing that a student may find is that there are few works specifically devoted to this particular subject.

The first key word in the title is *settlement* and it may be that there are a number of works on the importance of New York as a port of entry for migrants, but fewer devoted to the process whereby they settled in the city, and found work and housing. Nevertheless, books on the general topic would be useful. The second key word is *European*, and here it may be that most of the works found are devoted to migration from specific countries such as Poland or Germany. There may be fewer books which examine the broader issue of European migration in general. Although the project title specifically names New York, many of the references found may refer to settlement throughout the United States, rather than just within the New York area. Finally, many of the works consulted may not deal with the nineteenth century alone, but may examine migration during other periods.

The process of preparatory reading can often be somewhat frustrating. The exact type of books required may not seem to be available, and it may be necessary to spend a lot of time reading works only peripherally connected with the subject in question. Nevertheless, this can often be an indicator that the subject chosen for the project is fairly original. After all, if there were lots of readily available works on the exact subject, then it might indicate that the title had not been carefully chosen. You may also find a key text has already been borrowed from your college library so you may need to take availbility into account when planning your reading.

Organising your writing

Full-time students

Studying is never easy and all students, whether full-time or part-time need to manage their time effectively, to develop good study skills, and to organise their writing. Without sound planning, writing assignments can become an unnecessarily difficult chore. It is perhaps a paradox, but one of the difficulties for full-time students is that there often seems to be a great deal of time in which to complete an assignment. This can sometimes have two effects. One is to lull students into a false sense of security, so that they procrastinate with writing assignments. The other is that it creates a tendency to keep doing background reading and writing preparatory notes, but not actually writing the assignment. It may seem an obvious thing to say, but there are no marks for a partly completed assignment. Apart from adhering to the tutor's deadlines, it is often an advantage to create self-imposed deadlines for different stages of the work, and to try to stick to them.

Part-time students

For part-time students the situation with regard to study time is often quite the opposite. There may be the pressure of family and employment responsibilities, and finding the time to write assignments can be difficult. There is the need to recognise that although it might be possible to write a better essay given more time, it is important to complete the assignment rather than trying to strive after unattainable perfection.

The dilemma of the part-time student is that there is often a continual need to compromise between the limitations of time, and the motivation to produce the best possible piece of work. There is frequently the same dilemma in relation to preparatory reading. There always seems to be another important book to read, before writing can commence. As with full-time students though, time management is essential, and there comes that time when the reading has to stop, and the writing begin!

— The assessment of your work —

When a piece of work is submitted, it passes through a number of stages which could be as follows:

1 first marking and grading
2 second marking
3 internal moderation
4 external moderation
5 confirmation of award

For students this process may sometimes seem to be time consuming, but it has certain inbuilt safeguards which can provide reassurance that the assignment is being evaluated objectively.

On many programmes of study it is normal practice to assess pieces of work twice. The first marker writes comments on a proforma and allocates a particular grade. The work is then passed on to a second marker who may, or may not, have access to the first set of comments. When the second marker does not have access to the comments, the process is sometimes called 'blind' double marking. Sometimes a second comment sheet is completed, or alternatively the second marker simply countersigns the first comment sheet. If the two markers disagree about the grade, then there is usually an established mechanism to resolve the disagreement. This might involve a discussion between the two markers and the reaching of a compromise; or perhaps a more mathematical solution such as calculating the mean of the two grades. Whatever system is employed, the outcome is a comment sheet with an agreed grade, and signed by the two makers.

Although practices vary, it is sometimes possible for the student to be provided with feedback on the grade, at this stage. However, it has to be stressed that the grade is unconfirmed and could, in principle, be changed later. The reason for this is that individual tutors do not award credit or grades. It is only an official examining body or university that can award academic credit. Therefore, further stages in the process are necessary.

The next step is to conduct some form of comparative process within an institution to ensure that one tutor is not marking more generously or harshly than others. This so-called, internal moderation usually involves a number of tutors each reading work marked by their colleagues. Grades may sometimes be changed as a result of this process.

This process of moderation may be extended to compare work produced in one part of the country or at one institution, with that produced in other areas. This kind of process, usually termed external moderation, involves the participation of academics from areas or institutions some way removed from the work to be moderated. The purpose of this process is to seek to ensure the comparability of standards between different areas or institutions. The academics who carry out this function are termed external examiners or external moderators. Again, it is possible that grades can be changed as a result of this process.

The culmination of the process is a formal committee, often termed an 'exam board', at which results are presented and discussed by tutors and moderators. It is at this point that results are confirmed, and the outcome of the committee is a printed list which is then published in some form. When this list is available in the public domain, then the results are usually 'official'.

The details of the process will no doubt vary between organisations and between countries. However, this generalised system represents the essence of the assessment process, and its importance is that there are checks and balances which ensure fairness for the student. The system also produces feedback for the student and this is essential for academic development.

Getting feedback

Educational psychologists will confirm that getting feedback of results is an essential part of learning. A good assessment procedure generates detailed feedback comments for students. Even if a student has passed and obtained a good grade, it is often helpful to know exactly what has been done correctly, in order to reinforce this for the next assignment!

If an assignment has been allocated only a low grade then it is clearly important that the student should have a detailed statement setting out the failings of the piece of work, and the ways in which these can be improved.

> *PRACTICAL ADVICE*
>
> When you receive the comment sheet for an assignment, read it carefully. No matter whether you have done well or badly, make sure that you understand all of the comments.
>
> If you are in any doubt, consult your tutor and ask for clarification. It is better to be absolutely sure of how you can improve your work, than to make the same mistakes in subsequent assignments.

Summary

- Make sure that you have clear and precise aims for your assignment.
- Concentrate on developing your time management skills.
- Become familiar with the credit structure of your course.
- Read the assessment regulations for your course.
- Comply with word length and layout requirements of your assignment.
- Do not make the presentation style too ornate.
- Submit a detailed cover sheet with your assignment.
- Read your feedback or comment sheet carefully and consult your tutor if necessary.

3
THE ESSAY

— Selecting from a choice of titles —

One of the most crucial stages in writing an essay is the choice of title. Whether confronted with a choice of titles in an examination or for a coursework assignment, it is important to recognise that there are several different types of essay title which make different demands upon the writer. Although these general types of essay occur across most subject areas, it may be helpful to consider essay titles from one area, for example, the history of art. Here are four titles:

1. *Discuss the main features of a named art movement in the twentieth century.*
2. *What do you understand by the term 'art movement'? Name two artists who have contributed to the same movement, and for each trace their artistic development, indicating the main formative influences upon them.*
3. *Compare and contrast the contributions of Impressionism and Cubism to society in general.*
4. *'Painters just paint pictures. Art movements exist only in the minds of the critics.' Discuss.*

These essay titles differ in terms of length and detail, but in addition some are much more specific and focused in what they ask of the student.

The first essay is an example of a general title, which appears to leave a great deal of choice in the hands of the student. The second title is quite different. It is precise, requiring the student to address certain specified issues. Essay number three asks the student to make a comparison, and on first impression, may appear a fairly straightforward title. The last title requires considerable interpretive ability; first to understand the quotation, and then to employ existing knowledge to construct an interesting and well-argued discussion.

Even the apparently most straightforward of essays can be deceptively difficult and complex. It can demand subtle analytic skills which are not always evidently needed at a first rapid reading of the title. The above four essay titles are to some extent typical forms of essay. A consideration of each in turn shows both pros and cons for the student and the skills which may influence the choice.

1 The general essay

'Discuss the main features of a named art movement in the twentieth century.'

On the face of it, this essay appears to be straightforward. The only requirement seems to be the choice of a movement which rose to prominence during the twentieth century. Assuming a fairly detailed knowledge of one art movement, then the essay seems to be an attractive choice.

However, there is a disadvantage to this general type of title. There is absolutely no guidance to help with organising and structuring the essay. Everything is left up to the student. Before writing the essay, it is necessary to have a careful plan which identifies the 'main features' of the movement, and determines the order in which these will be discussed. A general essay such as this demands clear thinking and good organisational skills on the part of the writer.

2 The specific essay

'What do you understand by the term "art movement"? Name two artists who have contributed to the same movement, and for each trace their artistic development, indicating the main formative influences upon them.'

This is a much more specifically focused title, compared with the first one. The great advantage of this type of title is that it states much more precisely the structure of the essay, and the knowledge areas which must be demonstrated. There are far more points of guidance to enable the writer to plan the essay.

The disadvantage of this more specific essay is that the student has no choice but to answer the question. The first part of the title necessitates the student thinking out clearly the nature of the concept 'art movement'. There is no dodging this by writing about something on the periphery of the subject. Much the same is true of the rest of the question. It is not sufficient to think of two artists, and write a little about their lives. The question is self-evidently asking for something else. It stresses 'artistic development' and also 'formative influences'. Without the precise knowledge to discuss these topics, it might be better to choose another title.

3 The 'compare and contrast' essay

'Compare and contrast the contributions of Impressionism and Cubism to society in general.'

The advantage of this type of question is that it does provide a fairly precise instruction to the student, i.e. to draw a comparison. Some people may feel that this is preferable to a completely general and unstructured question.

However, there can be some difficulties with a title of this kind. For one thing, it demands a detailed knowledge of not one area, but of two. This is inevitable, if a comparison is to be drawn. This question may, therefore, require more knowledge than many other kinds of question. There is also the issue of the yardsticks by which the two movements will be contrasted. These must be clearly considered before essay writing commences.

4 The 'quotation' essay

'"Painters just paint pictures. Art movements exist only in the minds of the critics." Discuss.'

A good essay for those students with a broad understanding of their subject. Quotations can often be interpreted in a number of different ways, and the writer must explain the particular chosen meaning attributed to it. It can involve an analysis of the key concepts of the quotation, and the drawing together of knowledge and ideas from different aspects of a subject area.

This type of essay provides an excellent vehicle for knowledgeable students to display their understanding. This is an advantage for those who really know their subject. On the other hand, for those with a more limited grasp of their discipline, this type of question can be difficult to respond to adequately.

It would almost certainly be possible to think of other categories of essay title, which make different demands upon students. Perhaps the main lesson to learn from this discussion, is simply that essay titles require different treatment depending upon the way in which they are phrased. There are hidden subtleties in even the most apparently straightforward title, and it is essential in a good essay to explore these subtleties thoroughly.

Analysing the title

An essay title usually contains several key words, and it is crucial that a student responds to these in the structure of the essay. An example can be taken from a different subject area, such as sociology:

'What kind of behaviour can be described as deviant? What measures can society take in order to reduce the amount of deviant behaviour?'

The easiest way to analyse an essay title is to identify the 'key words', and then to ensure that the nuances of meaning of those words are fully appreciated. The key words in the above title are probably:

behaviour
deviant
measures
society
reduce
deviant behaviour

Each of these words has a significant impact upon the nature of the question, and must be addressed within the essay in order to provide a comprehensive response to the title. The first important aspect of the title, is that it asks for examples of deviant *behaviour* and not deviant *individuals*. The title does not personalise the issue of deviance, but rather makes a distinction between behaviour on the one hand, and those demonstrating that behaviour on the other. The concept of deviant behaviour is repeated at the end of the second part of the question.

The second key word is 'deviant' and in some ways this is the most important word in the title. Indeed, it is the real focus for the essay title. Now superficially, anything can be described as deviant, if it is different from the norm. This definition, however, begs many questions, including:

- How different does behaviour have to be before it can be described as deviant?
- What criteria can be used to define behavioural norms?
- Is it possible to define a norm?
- How are norms created in society?
- Which groups are in a position to be able to create a norm?

There are two polarised views of deviant behaviour. The first is that there are certain accepted standards of behaviour in society, and that anything different from those standards is deviant. On this view, the first part of the essay question is reasonably straightforward. It is possible to define the nature of deviance, and therefore to list examples of deviant behaviour.

There is, however, another interpretation of the concept 'deviant'. This is a much more subjective interpretation which sees deviant behaviour as being merely relative to a particular situation. Within this perspective, someone attending a rock concert dressed in a business suit is behaving just as deviantly as someone in rock gear attending a business convention. The deviance derives from a comparison with the context.

Now with this alternative interpretation of deviant behaviour, it is much more difficult to respond to the first part of the question. It would be necessary to analyse the concept of deviance, and then to point out that many different kinds of behaviour could be perceived as deviant, depending upon the context. In other words, the way in which the essay is approached depends upon the analysis of the key concepts in the title.

The second part of the title confronts the writer with similar problems. A quick reading suggests that the person who devised the question probably had in mind activities such as drug taking or squatting in unoccupied premises as examples of deviant behaviour. The question then becomes an evaluation of the possible steps society can take to reduce such activities or the laws which you feel might be passed to achieve certain aims. With this interpretation, the essay is probably fairly straightforward.

A more relative interpretation might argue that squatting, for example, is not necessarily deviant, but that it depends on the efforts the squatters have made to find more secure accommodation. It might also depend upon the extent of the help which they have received from various statutory agencies. In other words, the key concepts of 'measures', 'society' and 'reduce' could be seen as suggesting a punitive, law enforcing approach; or alternatively, could be perceived as indicating a supportive, understanding approach to behaviour which may not be totally conventional. You could also look at whether there is a different meaning attached to deviant behaviour in different societies and cultures.

The method used to analyse this title demonstrates that there are key words in a question which control the underlying meanings. There is frequently more than one way of interpreting an essay title, and more than one perspective from which the essay can be written. It is important to carry out this kind of interpretive analysis before writing commences. Having recognised that there is more than one interpretation of a title, there are probably two main strategies that the essay writer can adopt.

1 Select one particular viewpoint or perspective on the title, and explain this choice in the introduction to the essay. Having explained briefly that other perspectives are available, the remainder of the essay is written from the selected approach;

2 Write the entire essay from two or more perspectives, alternating between viewpoints in order to point out the complexity of some of the concepts. With this approach it is necessary to keep making it clear when there is a change of approach in the writing.

It is perfectly permissible to use either of these approaches in academic essays, although both have their potential dangers and drawbacks. In the first approach care must be taken to avoid appearing to be biased, or to have adopted an ideological position on an issue. In the second case, the reader of the essay can easily become confused with the changes in perspective in the essay.

PRACTICAL ADVICE

In the introduction to an essay, it is a good idea to explain clearly to the reader the particular approach you have taken. In this way, the reader knows what is coming, and can adjust to the structure of the essay. If we take as examples the two approaches discussed above, this is how you might introduce your essay:

> It is possible to view deviant behaviour in either absolutist terms or from a relativist point of view. The two approaches tend to lead to differing perceptions of the nature of deviance. This essay will adopt the absolutist perspective, and explore the insights which this brings to the reduction of deviance in society.

Alternatively, you could write:

> Deviant behaviour can be viewed from an absolute or a relative point of view. The first part of the essay examines the absolutist perspective, while the second explores the relativist viewpoint. The two approaches are contrasted in the conclusion.

Although it is possible to find much academic writing which adopts a single perspective, I feel that the second approach is preferable. It seems to me to encourage balance and objectivity. **Nevertheless, whichever approach you use, it is important for you to show that you understand the range of perspectives which exists**. After discussion with your tutor, try to adopt an approach which best meets the needs of the title.

As the above example was taken from the social sciences, it is worth pointing out some slight differences in essay writing within the natural sciences. As the previous discussion suggests, even the most apparently straightforward concepts in the social sciences can give rise to widely differing perspectives. This is much less so in biology or physics, where there is a more or less agreed corpus of knowledge as the basis of, for example, university entrance courses. Admittedly, much scientific data (e.g. at the sub-atomic level) does remain problematic to the extent that it is subject to differing interpretations, but there is in science a body of central, agreed concepts, which does not exist in the social sciences.

The effect of this is that essays on a scientific subject tend to be much more a systematic recounting of the 'facts' rather than, as in the social sciences, a discussion of ways of interpreting the world. However, science essays become much less factual and more discussional, where they concern the application of science to the world, or the ethics of science. Essays on environmental science can tend to be more discussional, for example, because they usually involve some degree of value judgement about the way in which science should be deployed.

The selection and analysis of the title are essential early stages in preparing an essay, but these thoughts need to be translated into a plan.

Preparing a plan

Having read the essay title and analysed the key words, the next stage is to decide the order in which to introduce ideas and issues. The preparation of a plan is crucial. Under examination conditions, this process has to take place rapidly and the results may not be written down, but merely retained in the mind. For a coursework essay, however, considerable time may be devoted to drafting and redrafting a suitable plan.

There is usually a variety of reasonable ways in which an essay may be structured. The following is an example of an environmental science essay:

Discuss the effects which industrial pollution is having on the environment.

A quick reading of the title, suggests that the key words are 'effects', 'industrial pollution', and 'environment'. These terms themselves suggest ways in which the essay might be structured.

It would be possible, for example, to consider different types of industrial pollution, and to discuss each in turn and the consequent effects upon the environment. Some of the examples which might be considered include emission of carbon dioxide and sulphur dioxide, deposition of chemical wastes, and unsafe disposal of radioactive waste. A plan for such an essay could be as follows:

1 Introduction to the nature of industrial pollution;
2 The causes of pollution;
3 Types of industrial pollution and their effects:
- noise pollution
- chemical pollution
- radioactive pollution
- oxides of carbon and sulphur
- plastics and packaging disposal

4 Extent of the effects;
5 Timescale for the effects;
6 Conclusion: possible remedial measures.

The first two sections of the essay would set the scene, explaining the nature of industrial pollution and the pressures, economic and otherwise, which result in pollution. This would be followed by a systematic examination of the different types of industrial pollution and their effects. This is the main part of the essay and would contain the principal body of evidence and references. Three concluding sections would follow, on the scale of pollution, on future projections for pollution levels, and on measures which might be taken to reduce the effects of pollution.

The plan has the advantage of examining the title systematically, and of providing a framework to help the essay writer. Each numbered section could consist of a paragraph or group of paragraphs, depending upon the required length of the essay.

However, there are other possibilities for developing a plan for this particular essay title. It would be possible to consider the key word of 'environment' and to review the pollution effects upon different aspects of the ecosystem. The plan could be as follows:

1 Introduction to industrial pollution;
2 The 'balance' of the environment;
3 The effects of pollution in:
- the air and atmosphere
- rivers and lakes
- the sea
- the land

(with particular reference in each case to plant and animal life)

4 Conclusion: future strategies to minimise pollution effects.

Although the plan addresses the title differently, it retains a systematic approach within which it would be possible for the writer to present the key ideas for the essay.

> ### *PRACTICAL ADVICE*
>
> When you are developing a plan for an essay, take one of the key concepts in the title, and subdivide it into sections. Each of these sections should be suitable for a paragraph or group of paragraphs.
>
> If you find that one particular concept does not subdivide conveniently, try another one. You will usually find that a reasonable plan emerges from this process. Then add one or two introductory and concluding sections, and the plan should be ready for writing.

Surveying the literature

The purpose and style of referring to relevant academic literature in an essay is rather different to that in a research report. First, the essay title will normally be somewhat more general than the subject for a research report, and therefore the range of literature covered will be broader in scope, but less detailed. Essay references may be less concerned with the details of experimental procedures and results. It may simply be a matter of referring to a leading writer in the field, and summarising, in one or two sentences, the essence of what was discovered or emerged from research. In an essay there may also be fewer references than in a research report. The essay is more concerned with the exploration and interrelationship of ideas, than with the collection and analysis of data. There is often rather less need to refer continually to previous research.

Inevitably, there will also be a difference in the extent of referencing in an examination essay and in a coursework essay. In an examination it may be possible to remember one or two brief quotations to use, but generally references will take the form of naming a key writer and perhaps the year in which the main work was produced. In a coursework essay, on the other hand, there is plenty of time to collate references and to employ them in detail throughout the text. In certain special cases, such as the study of literature involving the detailed reading of a set book, it may be quite natural to learn long passages, and these are then available to use for reference purposes in examinations.

A survey of the literature is an essential precursor to writing an essay, simply in order to ensure familiarity with the subject matter. There are, however, other purposes in understanding the literature and in referring to it in essays, and these vary from subject to subject. A number of these reasons are set out below, along with the subject areas in which they are particularly relevant.

1 To demonstrate that the writer of the essay has read widely and has a broad appreciation of the subject matter

In a psychology essay, for example, this might take the form of naming key researchers who have made significant contributions. In business studies or management studies it may be important to name leading theorists in the field and also those who have made contributions through empirical work.

2 To document the sequential development of knowledge and understanding in a particular field

In a law essay it may be necessary to refer to the development of legal precedents in a particular area. Alternatively, in history there is frequently the need to demonstrate that historians are able to revise our interpretation of historical events as new evidence comes to light. In science the progress of a particular idea may be illustrated by reference to major events like the discovery of the structure of DNA and its subsequent use in crime detection.

3 To provide illustrative examples of a particular theme

In an essay on poetry, for example, it might be necessary to select examples from individual poets to illustrate a stylistic device such as alliteration. The same may well be true of essays on literature in general, in English or in other languages. Another example, could be sociology where an essay could involve a discussion of different types of authority, including charismatic authority. It may be necessary to refer to some charismatic leaders and their work, in order to illustrate this theme.

4 As a device to introduce a discussion within the essay

Philosophy essays are a good example of this. Generally such essays tend to have relatively few quotations, as they consist primarily of logical argument and conceptual clarification. However, it is often useful to take a single, interesting quotation which involves problematic conceptual issues, and to subject it to analytic scrutiny.

5 In order to substantiate the essay writer's arguments

This is perhaps the most common reason for references and quotations. Typically, the writer wishes to argue a particular case, which might be that participation rates in higher education are increasing. There would then be references to official and governmental publications in order to support the general contention. The referencing may take the form of simply naming an author in the text, and referring to the full work in the bibliography. Alternatively, the writer may employ actual extracts or quotations. References for this purpose are used in a wide range of subject essays, from biology to economics, and sociology to theology.

Referencing then, is a basic technique in writing academic essays, but it is important for the cohesion of the essay to select suitable quotations.

Selecting quotations

The simplest form of reference does not employ a quotation as such. This occurs where there is a need in an essay merely to indicate a particular book or journal article. For example, it might be necessary to say:

> A leading writer in this field is Smith (1995) who has written the definitive history of the event.

The full details of the work would be provided in the bibliography. This type of referencing is easy to use and is useful for indicating a broad familiarity with an academic area.

In other cases, it may be necessary to include in the essay a verbatim extract from a book or article. Where this is done, it is probably best to consider the following issues:

- The quotation should not be too long;
- It should be relevant and fulfil its purpose in the essay;
- It should not break unduly the flow of the prose.

An essay is intended to be primarily the work of the writer, and quotations should be used to the minimum. They should not be used with such frequency that they interfere with the flow of ideas, and make the prose appear disjointed. In addition it is necessary to describe the exact origin of the quotation, so that, if necessary, the reader can find it in the original context. There are certain formal conventions for doing this, and these are described in Chapter 8.

Incorporating theory

Inevitably, an essay consists mostly of the writer's views and opinions. This is as it should be, but if an essay consists of this alone, then it will be somewhat limited in scope. The arguments in the essay will be based upon the life experience of the writer, and the logical generalisations which can be drawn from this. While it is obviously better to choose a subject about which you can argue cogently, be careful about pursuing 'hobby horses' to the extent you lose track of the title actually set.

However, the use of 'theory' in an essay broadens out the evidence upon which arguments can be based. There is a common misconception about theory and theories, that they are invented by thinkers and academics in their own minds, without reference to the real world. This is simply not so. All theory is based upon observations; or, to put it slightly more technically, 'empirical evidence'. Theories are developed by making precise observations, and then by developing a general statement which links together those observations, explains them to some extent, and tries to predict the kind of observations which might be made in the future. This general statement is the theory. These issues are discussed in more detail in Chapter 9, but for now, an example from psychology will illustrate how theory can help in an essay.

Psychologists have lots of ideas about the things which drive human beings to behave as they do, or to take certain actions. In other words, there are a number of different explanations for 'motivation'. If we had to write an essay on motivation without recourse to theory, then it would be necessary to either reflect on our own motivational drives, or recount what others had told us. It might also be possible to make a few logical deductions about the kinds of things which do motivate people.

On the other hand, reference to a general theory provides us with a mechanism to discuss far more situations involving motivation. Abraham Maslow, an American psychologist, developed a theory of motivation which is probably familiar to most students of introductory psychology. In short, this theory suggested a hierarchy of basic human needs, starting with physiological needs such as food and air, passing through needs such as safety and affection, and ending with the need to attain some kind of self-fulfilment. Maslow's suggestion is that most human beings are motivated to act in order to satisfy the basic needs of food and clothing first, and only then to try to satisfy the 'higher order' needs. The theory was not just 'an idea', but was based upon extensive empirical data.

A theory such as this enables the essay writer to link together a variety of different situations and also to try to explain them within a coherent framework. For example, we might consider the case of someone who gets up late for work one morning, gets dressed, snatches a quick cup of coffee, and rushes off, without the normal conversation and pleasanteries. Within Maslow's theory, this would be explained by suggesting that the person was primarily motivated by the need to succeed at work and hence earn the money to satisfy basic needs such as food and clothing.

Perhaps the same individual devotes a great deal of the weekend to membership of an amateur theatre group. This might be explained by suggesting that having met the basic physiological needs, more time can be devoted to acting because this satisfies needs associated with gaining recognition and self-fulfilment. In other words, a good theory can be applied acrosss a wide range of human experience, and used to explain and interpret diverse events.

A good essay will treat issues not only at the individual level, but will use theory to examine events on a broader plane. It is worth noting, however, that theories, particularly in the social sciences, cannot be regarded as providing the final, ultimate explanation of events. Theories are always provisional, and subject to the collection of new data which causes them to be superseded.

PRACTICAL ADVICE

When you mention a theory in your essay, it is best to remember that a theory is only as good as the latest evidence which supports it. There is always the chance that something will occur which will contradict the theory. It is, therefore, always wise to be cautious in your writing style. For example:

> Maslow's hierarchy of needs is a helpful model for trying to understand human motivation.

or

> Maslow's theory provides a useful framework for seeking to explain the variety of human motivation.

In both cases there is a tentative element to the means of expression.

– Presenting different perspectives –

In some areas of life, society tends to expect people to have firm views about things. If we think of perhaps party politicians or senior managers of large organisations, it is often the case that they are expected to think out an issue clearly and then to express their viewpoint forthrightly. They might even be thought to be ineffectual if they express uncertainty about an issue, or perhaps keep changing their minds.

However, the situation with academic writers is different. Many will interpret evidence in a particular way and will, therefore, tend to write from a specific perspective. There is much more of a tendency to acknowledge other views and possible interpretations. This is not seen as weakness or prevarication, but rather as a willingness to see both or all sides of an issue. As long as it is clear that the writer has analysed the competing viewpoints, it would generally be seen as an academic virtue to perceive the full range of possible interpretations inherent in a situation.

An example of the importance of multiple perspectives is in the interpretation of historical events and, in particular, the causation of historical events. It is generally difficult to attribute a single cause to an event. Even multiple causes can be difficult to substantiate. The problem is that the notion of 'cause', implying an event which brings another event into existence, is difficult to establish. It is much safer to think in terms of 'factors' which influence events.

For example, a perhaps simplistic view of the Norman invasion of England in 1066, would be that William invaded because King Harold had not honoured his oath to support William's claim to the English throne. To view this as the 'cause' of the Norman invasion would, however, be too reductionist. It would be better to view this as one of a number of factors including:

- the military development of Normandy
- the personalities of William and Harold
- the extent of the expansionist ambitions of William
- the relationship between England and Norway
- the economic status of England, and its desirability as a conquest

There are no doubt many other factors which could be postulated, but the most appropriate stance to take is that all of the factors interacted in a complex way, with the result that the Duke of Normandy decided to invade England.

Now it may be that in this case, or indeed any other, it is felt that one particular factor was pre-eminent. It is then perfectly acceptable to state this in the essay. Having reviewed the various factors concerned, the writer can come to the conclusion that one particular factor was more important than the others. The important thing, in this case, is to set down clearly the reasons for coming to this conclusion. It is essential to show that evidence has been carefully evaluated.

— How to select and present evidence —

Unlike a research report, an essay is not concerned with the detailed analysis of evidence. An essay tends to be more of an opportunity for the writer to present an adept argument for or against a particular case, or to analyse a contentious issue in a detailed and comprehensive way. To this end, it is less essential to quote primary data. There are three main types of evidence which are useful to incorporate in an essay: the authoritative source; empiral data; analysis of concepts.

The authoritative source

This is where an argument is substantiated by reference to a leading academic, writer or public figure who has gone on record as supporting the particular argument proposed by the essay writer. For example:

> This particular economic policy was continually supported by the new Prime Minister for the duration of the administration.

Authoritative sources can also be organisations. For example:

> The previously mentioned international charity concurs with this view about the distribution of resources in developing countries.

Arguments do not become true, simply because an authoritative figure agrees with them. It is, however, a useful step in beginning to establish a particular case.

Empirical data

It is possible to seek to establish the truth of an argument, by basing it upon empirical data. This can be primary data, collected in person by the essay writer; or secondary data, such as statistical material collected by others. In both cases, the data includes material collected by such methods as experiments, surveys or interviews. For example:

Traffic flow rates on our urban road system vary considerably with different weather conditions. In an officially sponsored research study five main arterial roads were regularly monitored in widely different weather situations.

The empirical data does not make the statement in the essay correct. The reader of the essay must make judgements about the value of the data, and about its relevance to the case raised in the essay.

Analysis of concepts

Sometimes in an essay, it is useful to try to establish an argument by recourse to the ideas and principles allegedly contained within a concept.

For example, in an essay which is exploring aspects of medical ethics, a writer may say:

> It is contrary to the entire notion of a doctor that a patient, irrespective of the degree of illness, should be helped to die. Life and death are not the gift of a medical practitioner. Only God can so intervene.

This argument is not supported by either a claim to authority, or empirical data. It is suggested that doctors should not be involved in euthanasia, simply because it is alien to the idea of practising medicine. It is furthermore suggested, that only God has the authority to determine the moment of death. These are conceptual arguments because they depend for their veracity or otherwise, upon the differing ideas held of the nature of 'being a doctor' and of the nature of 'God'. The problem with the use of these arguments is that people frequently differ in their interpretation of the same concept. An example is 'justice'. This is a well-known concept, and one to which most people would probably claim to subscribe. Nevertheless, it is still frequently notoriously difficult to gain a consensus on what is a 'just' course of action in particular circumstances. A specific conceptual argument can, therefore, be plausible to one person, but quite fallacious to another.

Using anecdotes and personal experience

One of the main purposes of presenting evidence in an essay is to enable the reader to evaluate that evidence and, therefore to decide on the validity of the writer's argument. The basic difficulty in employing subjective experience as evidence is that it is difficult, if not impossible, for another person to verify that evidence. Suppose, for example, that in an essay discussing the car industry in Europe, someone writes:

> The French tend to have a definite preference for buying French cars. When I have been to France, I see very few foreign cars, usually only French models.

The initial assertion may, or may not, be true; but the problem with the evidence is that it is limited. The writer can inevitably have seen only a minority of all cars in France. The writer's experience might, in fact, be replicated over the whole country, but we simply do not know this, and cannot really build any kind of argument upon it.

There are, however, certain subject areas where subjective experience may be valuable to support an argument. In general, subject areas which involve a degree of aesthetic or artistic interpretation can provide a forum where personal views and experience have a legitimate role to play. In discussing a painting or a musical composition it may be perfectly relevant to describe the effect that the art work has on oneself. The reason for this being acceptable in this context is that, arguably, art and music are always interpreted on the individual level. The case might be made that it is only on the subjective level that art can be understood. Other similar subject areas could be the interpretation of architecture, poetry, and literature in general.

These are really philosophical issues, but it is at least possible that personal experience has a legitimate part to play as evidence in such discussion. This is not, however, the case with the next issue.

Avoiding plagiarism

Plagiarism is the act of incorporating the writing of someone else in an assignment, without acknowledging the actual source. This must be wrong in principle, and in many institutions there are specific policies setting out a variety of sanctions against students who are demonstrated to have plagiarised the work of another person.

The quoting of passages from another work is not plagiarism, as long as the details of the author and work are noted in full. The procedure for doing this is discussed in detail in Chapter 8.

One potential problem with the extensive reading which is often required in order to write an academic essay is that it is frequently necessary to read and then reread a passage, in order to grasp the meaning. During this process it can easily happen that certain key phrases and expressions become part of the short-term memory, and are transferred to the essay being written. This could not fairly be described as plagiarism, which is normally taken to involve the intentional copying of a substantial, continuous extract. However, it is possible to minimise the inadvertent use of phrases from the original, and at the same time, to learn more thoroughly the material which is being read.

PRACTICAL ADVICE

When you are studying a passage prior to writing an essay, read the section carefully several times, and try to make sure that you fully understand the ideas which are discussed. Try to apply the ideas to your own experience. Think of new examples of the ideas, other than the ideas given in the passage. Analyse the ideas, trying to work out if they seem logical.

Then put the book on one side for a few minutes, and do something different. When you return to write the relevant section of the essay, you should find that you genuinely describe the ideas in your own words.

– Your tutor's view or your own view? –

Teachers are like anyone else – they have their own interests, their favourite topics for discussion, and their own opinions about the contentious issues of the day. Within their own academic discipline, they may have their own preferred perspective and their own preferred research method. When it comes to matters of interpreting evidence, an individual tutor may prefer one interpretation to the others which are possible. When students write essays they can sometimes be uncertain whether or not to try to reflect the apparent preference of their tutor. They may feel that they should trust the judgement of their tutor.

Now this apparent dilemma is not really a dilemma at all. The crucial thing for a student is to distinguish between procedural advice involving essay layout and ways of presenting arguments, and on the other hand, advice concerning the interpretation of data. In the case of the latter, in particular, it is important that students apply their own critical and analytical faculties to a problem. If this means that they come to a different conclusion to their tutor, then so be it. In this case, in the essay, it will be essential to provide the supporting reasons for the argument or stance which is taken, but then to argue the issue with conviction.

> *PRACTICAL ADVICE*
>
> When you are confronted with a complex matter of interpretation of data, read widely around the subject and listen to conflicting opinions. Then make up your own mind, and express your opinion with conviction, giving a precise account of the supporting reasons.

— Checking, correcting and editing —

The assumption behind this section is that a word processor is being used, although some of the comments would apply equally to the editing of a rough, handwritten copy of an essay.

It is not easy to read and correct text directly on the computer screen. It is preferable to print a paper copy of the essay, and correct that. When the editing is complete, then the changes can be made on the disk, and a final copy printed. (Don't forget to backup your disk with the final version.)

In some ways it is easier to correct the first printout in stages. It can be difficult to read a draft essay, and simultaneously look out for spelling, punctuation, stylistic and content errors. It can be easier to read through the essay looking for only one category of error at a time. One way to do this is first to consider only content issues, such as the sequence of the paragraphs and the ways in which arguments are presented. It can be easier at this stage to ignore temporarily any grammatical errors. The following is a checklist of possible content issues:

- Does the introduction adequately set the scene for a new reader?
- Does the introduction provide an overview of the structure of the essay?
- Are the paragraphs balanced in length?
- Is each paragraph devoted to a single idea or issue...?
- Are the paragraphs and ideas sequenced correctly?
- Are arguments logical and adequately supported with relevant evidence?
- Does the conclusion draw together the main issues?

- Does the conclusion either reach a compromise view, or arrive at a particular viewpoint that is substantiated by evidence?
- Most importantly, does the essay answer the question in the title?

Having checked the content of the essay, it is a good idea to make sure that certain structural matters are correct. Examples are:

- Is it long enough?
- Are extracts quoted referenced in the bibliography?
- Is the bibliography in alphabetical order?
- Is the referencing system consistent?
- Are margins and page numbers correct?
- Is the title page or cover sheet set out with necessary information?
- Do the headings reflect what the text is about and do they match the contents list?
- Are the tables or diagrams in the best place in the text and are they numbered correctly?
- Does the data in the tables/diagrams tally with the text?

Finally, spelling errors, grammar and punctuation can be corrected. This process of correcting in stages may seem lengthy and tedious. If so, then editing and correcting can all be carried out in one stage. The method which seems most appropriate may depend on the extent of the corrections to be made. If the corrections are extensive, it may be easier and more accurate to deal with them in stages. Minor corrections may be remedied more easily in a single process.

— How will your essay be assessed? —

It is desirable that students are given full information about the mechanism for assessing their essays. This includes factors such as:

- Whether the essay will be marked by one tutor or two tutors (i.e. 'single marked' or 'double marked');
- If 'double marked', the procedure for reconciling different marks for the same essay;
- The assessment criteria;
- The grading scale; a literal scale, using letters, or a percentage;
- The way in which feedback will be provided. This is usually by written comments on an assessment proforma;
- The timescale for completing the marking;

- The date of the 'examination board' when the grade or credit is officially recorded;
- The nature of the referral system, whereby the essay can be resubmitted if it does not pass at the first assessment;
- Whether the essay will be returned to the student, or retained

This kind of information is usually freely available to students, but may be in fairly detailed documents like course handbooks, which are lodged in a library. It is always worth asking for the information, as much of it can be important for the student.

Marking schemes and assessment criteria

The assessment criteria are the standards by which the essay is judged. These standards are normally available to students in order that they can meet the assessment requirements. They include:

- The essay should cover the main areas of relevant subject matter and discuss and evaluate these in an objective manner;
- The essay should be written in lucid prose, enabling arguments to be presented logically and systematically;
- The concluding paragraphs should summarise the arguments and evidence, and direct the reader towards a systematic conclusion or synthesis of the ideas;
- The essay should address the questions and issues posed.

Such criteria enable the assessor to form a judgement about the quality of the essay. Sometimes the criteria such as those above are interpreted in order to arrive at a grade or percentage band on the grading scale. Alternatively, there may be different criteria for each separate mark band on the grading scale.

Assessment criteria help to make the process of assessing essays more systematic. The other strategy which is used either in conjunction with criteria or alone, is that of the marking scheme. This involves the identification of those aspects of knowledge, and those forms of argument which are seen as desirable to include in the essay. Each particular element is allocated a mark in advance, and the student accumulates marks by in mentioning the key points. There may also be marks for those more general aspects mentioned in the criteria above.

It is important that students understand the procedure for marking essays so that they can write in the desired format and style.

The tutor's perfect essay!

Presumably, such a piece of writing does not exist, but certain features of an essay really help tutors, particularly when they are assessing a large number of essays.

Clarity of writing style is important. It can be frustrating to have to read and then re-read parts of an essay because the style is rather convoluted and it is difficult to follow the arguments. The essay style and structure should be straightforward, and such that the reader can read the essay at one go, and understand immediately the key arguments and issues which are raised.

An area which is well within the control of the student is that of typing errors, unnecessary spelling mistakes, and basic grammar. These errors can be distracting when reading an essay, and can easily detract from the quality of an otherwise sound piece of writing. Careful checking can minimise such errors.

A final point is the virtue of adhering to the title. Essays which wander from the title cause assessment difficulties for the tutor. If there is the temptation to interpret the title rather liberally, then it is essential to explain carefully the rationale for this.

Summary

- Select the essay title carefully.
- Choose the kind of essay which you enjoy writing.
- Identify the key words in the title and respond to these as you write.
- Plan the essay – even if only in your mind.
- Produce a clear introduction followed by lucid prose.
- When writing the essay, keep the future reader in mind.
- Try to imagine how the future reader will respond to the essay.
- Take care with referencing and the bibliography.
- Make sure that you present a balanced view of issues.
- Have confidence in your own analysis of ideas.
- Check and edit the essay carefully.

4
THE PORTFOLIO

What is a portfolio?

Traditionally, art and design students collect drawings and designs in a large portfolio. In current educational terms, a portfolio is a collection of evidence that an individual has acquired knowledge, or has developed skills or work competence.

The portfolio has come to prominence in the areas of work-based training and vocational education. It is particularly used, for example, in the National Vocational Qualifications in England. The adaptability of the portfolio is also making it increasingly attractive as a means of assessment in Higher Education.

There is no reason why the portfolio cannot be used on academic programmes. In this respect its use is spreading rapidly, particularly in relation to the accreditation of prior learning. Students in many areas of education are increasingly encouraged to submit evidence of learning which they have previously acquired, in order to gain some preliminary credit on a programme, and thus not need to start at the beginning of the course. The portfolio is normally employed as the vehicle through which the evidence can be assembled and submitted.

What does it contain?

A portfolio can be a voluminous collection of material or simply consist of one or two brief documents. It may also 'contain' artefacts such as sculpture and objects manufactured in engineering or craft, design and technology. The portfolio may also make reference to large-scale objects which are non-transportable. These might include, for example, a wall built by a construction student. Photographs of the wall in various stages of construction might be included in the portfolio.

The purpose of the portfolio is to provide evidence of learning and skill acquisition. To this end there are perhaps some typical categories of material which could be included:

Essays, laboratory reports, lecture notes, tape recordings of discussion groups, seminar papers, dissertations, and research data
These and other items could provide evidence of academic learning. The documentary evidence might need to be supplemented by a test or examination to demonstrate that the learning is still current. This is particularly important if the evidence was prepared or accumulated some time in the past.

Certificates and diplomas relating to qualifications
Certificates and diplomas could be for major or minor qualifications. They may be submitted because parts of the curriculum studied are relevant to the new qualification for which the portfolio is concerned. It may also be appropriate to include copies of the syllabus or course document which has been studied.

References from responsible people who can attest to the knowledge or skill of an individual
These might consist of the actual references which have been written. Alternatively, the names, addresses and occupations of those willing to provide a reference could be included.

Offers by the compiler of the portfolio to be directly assessed on a particular topic
The proposed assessments might take the form of a written examination, a viva voce, or participation in a discussion. The idea behind this possibility is that people can acquire skills and knowledge in a variety of ways, not necessarily within a formalised academic or training establishment.

Arguably, the most important thing is that the individual actually possesses the knowledge and skills, and can demonstrate these in an assessment setting.

Evidence of attending short courses, in-house training, staff development sessions, and appraisal interviews

There is a wide range of potential evidence here, most of which is likely to apply primarily to mature students who have been in employment. Employees in many jobs and professions are encouraged to take part in short courses of professional development, which may be as short as half a day in length. Often these courses do not lead to a qualification. If the employee has maintained records of the work covered, and also of any assessments, then this can be useful evidence for a portfolio.

Similarly, work-based appraisal sessions are normally supported by summaries of the achievements during the previous year. This summary, or the appraiser's report after the interview, can constitute important evidence of knowledge and skill acquisition.

Artefacts

Artefacts can be extremely important in skill areas such as joinery and catering. In some cases, such as catering, it may be impractical to save the actual product, but other means of recording such as photographs can be used. In this case, it will probably be essential to include an official statement testifying that the named individual carried out the specified work.

Writing and publications

There is no reason why this should include only commercially published material such as books or articles. It could include any non-published material which has had limited circulation; letters to newspapers; newsletter contributions; articles in professional or trade journals; fictional writing of any kind.

Documents produced in an official capacity and/or at work

There is an extensive range of potential material here. Some possibilities include correspondence, minutes of meetings, discussion documents, research proposals, official reports, financial estimates, and records of technical tests.

Some of this material may be confidential, and may require the deletion of names to preserve anonymity. It may also be necessary to seek official permission before including such documents in a portfolio.

These eight categories of material are not exhaustive but they indicate the wide range of examples of evidence which can be included in a portfolio. Much of this type of material relates to the world of work and to the development of vocational and technical skills. Portfolios are thus being seen as increasingly relevant to the situation of mature and 'access' students who have already had one or more careers before deciding to pursue academic study further. Evidence can also be chosen which indicates the acquisition of knowledge which supports technical skill learning. In this way, it is possible to relate vocational experience to academic courses, and so enable mature students to gain credit for their previous learning at work.

When you complete your portfolio it is essential that everything in it is clearly marked (by means, for example, of a label on the reverse) with your name and home or college address.

Learning outcomes and performance criteria

The use of portfolios is particularly relevant on programmes where learning is expressed in terms of 'outcomes'. Traditionally, educational programmes have been described in terms of a syllabus, or summary statement of the main topics to be studied. The difficulty with a syllabus is that it does not prescribe any particular level or depth of study. For example, 'British history between the two World Wars' might conceivably be part of a history syllabus in a high school or at a university. It is impossible to know, simply from the name of the topic.

Learning outcomes are a much more precise means of describing the learning process. They state the exact skills or abilities which individuals are expected to possess at the end of the programme. For example, one learning outcome of a computing course might be: 'The student can use a word processing package to type a business letter.'

This is a precise statement, illustrating several features of learning outcomes. First, it is clearly possible to measure this outcome. At the end of the programme, the student could be asked to type a particular letter using a word processing package. The student could be observed and the final letter examined.

The second feature of learning outcomes is that they are independent of the learning process or learning context. In other words, we are not concerned here with how the student managed to be able to type the business letter, merely that the student demonstrably possessed the ability. The skills might, for example, have been acquired in a conventional class and taught by a tutor; or they could have been learned from a self teaching computer package. This aspect of learning outcomes is important in relation to portfolios, because it is merely necessary to provide evidence of meeting the outcome, rather than any background evidence describing the location of learning. The latter may, indeed, have taken place at home, or at the workplace, or in a training or educational establishment.

Outcomes can be described in terms of the learning of new knowledge, or the learning of new skills. The typing of a business letter, for example, involves both knowledge and skills. An example of a knowledge outcome would be: 'The student can describe two different conventions for the layout of a business letter.' This is a knowledge outcome, because the student must learn the two conventions and describe them, but is not necessarily required to type letters illustrating these conventions. On the other hand, a skill outcome would be: 'The student can type directly from an audio tape recording.' There is no significant knowledge element here, but primarily a matter of skill development.

Not only can learning outcomes be demonstrated, but it is possible for one individual to achieve a learning outcome more effectively or efficiently than someone else. In order to illustrate this, we can reconsider the original outcome:

'The student can use a word-processing package to type a business letter.' This outcome statement does not include, in its present form, any mention of the quality of the business letter which is produced. There is no mention of standard of work. In fact, the typing of a business letter can be carried out according to a number of different criteria:

- speed of typing
- accuracy with which the original is typed
- design and layout of the letter
- efficiency of the filing system on the computer disk
- quality of the printing

There may be other important criteria, particularly if we consider the context of a busy office environment. A typist or secretary may be under considerable pressure to take a message or to send a fax, while in the middle of typing a letter to meet a deadline. The ability to work to high standards in this kind of environment is part of work competence. To type an accurate business letter while under work pressure, may well be another important criterion.

These criteria can be rephrased in order to write 'performance criteria' for the particular outcome. In relation to the above outcome, several performance criteria might be:

1 An average letter of approximately 150 words can be typed and printed in 10 minutes;
2 Letters only rarely contain copying errors;
3 A systematic computer file of letters is maintained, with facility for rapid retrieval.

When compiling a portfolio it is helpful to have available both the learning outcomes and the performance criteria of the course or programme for which the portfolio is being submitted. In this way, the evidence for the portfolio can be carefully selected and annotated.

– Selecting and matching evidence –

When selecting evidence for the portfolio, the main requirement is that the material should relate to the learning outcomes and performance criteria. This is the first of three important requirements for portfolio evidence. These are:

- relevance
- sufficiency
- currency

In relation to the above outcome concerning the typing of a letter, it is probably fairly clear when some evidence would be irrelevant. A sample of desktop publishing would not be relevant because there are distinctive skills associated with the business letter. The criterion of sufficiency may sometimes be difficult to satisfy. Simply providing a sample of a single letter would not be sufficient. One might argue as a sceptic that the letter could have been typed by someone else. A reference from an office manager stating that the candidate had excellent typing skills would be an improvement on the evidence. Perhaps the only completely sufficient evidence, would be a willingness to undertake a typing test.

This evidence would also satisfy the final criterion of currency. This criterion is concerned with the extent to which the evidence still applies to the candidate. It is concerned with the issue of whether knowledge and skills acquired by the candidate some time ago, are still possessed at the present time. An oral or written examination, or a practical test are effective methods of determining currency. However, the assessors of the portfolio may not wish to apply tests to all candidates. It is preferable if at least some evidence can be provided of currency within the actual portfolio.

Letters of commendation or references which refer to recently demonstrated skills, are a useful source of evidence. This is particularly so if they are dated and refer to events on specified dates. Currency might also be suggested by the inclusion of a computer disk containing examples of dated letters, where the letters also refer to events on specified dates.

It is preferable not to include so much evidence, that the portfolio becomes difficult to handle and daunting to examine. The goal should be to include adequate evidence, but in a quantity which is accessible and can be readily absorbed by the assessor. There can be a temptation to include a mass of evidence, in order to meet all the criteria and outcomes. The approach should be one of parsimony compatible with relevance, sufficiency and currency.

— Choosing appropriate artefacts —

Artefacts can include a variety of prepared or manufactured objects which suggest the possession of skill in the student or candidate. They might include a sculpture, a piece of furniture or an electrical circuit on a circuit board. The problem with all artefacts is that it is important to demonstrate that they were actually made by the candidate. Supplementary evidence is therefore required.

This kind of evidence might include a brief statement explaining the history of the artefact, and the way in which it was manufactured. The statement could also include a summary of the skills which either had to be acquired prior to manufacture, or were gained during the manufacture process. There could also be photographs of the different stages of construction.

Some artefacts may be too large to transport. Candidates who have been employed in building trades, for example, can scarcely bring along the products of their labours. They may however, possess photographs of buildings or architectural drawings which would indicate the scale and character of projects in which they have been involved.

A portfolio should be seen in a creative sense, and there are no real conventions as to the appearance of the portfolio nor as to what it should contain. The student or candidate should not forget, however, the assessment process, and that someone eventually will have to evaluate the material.

Obtaining new evidence

If for some reason, evidence is not regarded as sufficient to support a claim to have met a learning outcome, then more relevant evidence will be required. It is sometimes worth analysing possible evidence in terms of the closeness of the connection with the outcome. Some evidence can be regarded as 'primary' and some as 'secondary'.

Primary evidence is where the assessor can actually see the candidate performing a skill or listen to someone discussing an idea. There can be no question in such cases, that the candidate possesses the knowledge and skills concerned. If a student discusses the concept of 'social status' in a sociology class, and can answer questions on the topic coherently, then there can be little question that the topic is understood. This is primary evidence. If a student is observed assembling a high frequency radio receiver, then this is primary evidence. An essay on social status or the actual radio receiver would not constitute primary evidence. These would be secondary evidence because there is no empirical connection with the student concerned. Further evidence would be required to establish the connection with the student.

It is never easy to assemble absolute evidence in a portfolio. The student should assemble material which can reasonably establish the completion of learning outcomes.

Obtaining references and testimonials

These two terms are to some extent interchangeable, but can be distinguished as follows:

A *reference* is a statement concerning a student's abilities or knowledge, which is written in connection with a specific object or intention. This can be a job application, or in this case the attainment of learning outcomes. The reference is often addressed to a named person or organisation. It is frequently confidential to the writer and addressee. The student may not see its contents unless there are specific arrangements to the contrary.

A *testimonial* is a general statement concerning a student, but one which is not addressed to a specific person. It is available to the student to copy and distribute as wished.

When trying to assemble references or testimonials, it is important to consider the type of person who should be approached, and the kind of information which is required in the reference. These are the main stages in the process:

1. Select the outcomes for which evidence is required;
2. Make a list of individuals who are in a position to affirm that these outcomes have been met;
3. Select one or two people who would probably be willing to help. Other things being equal, select individuals who are in a position of significant responsibility;
4. Write a carefully worded letter (see below) explaining the purpose of the reference and particularly the skills and knowledge which it is hoped the referee will mention. The quality of the reference may depend largely upon the precision of the letter.

Always remember that the person you ask for a reference is probably very busy. It will certainly not harm your prospects of a good reference if you show you are grateful for their time and trouble. A small company or organisation may well appreciate a stamped, addressed, envelope as well.

PRACTICAL ADVICE

When you ask for a reference or testimonial, your letter could be something like this:

Dear ....

As you know I have recently embarked on a BA(Hons) in Theatre Studies. I am really enjoying it and the experience I gained with the South England Theatre Company has proved very useful. One of the early modules is concerned with stage design and I have been told that I do not have to do this module if I prepare a portfolio of the work I have done for the Theatre Company. I have got together my drawings for the designs I did over the last three years, and also some photographs of productions. I just need to have evidence of practical skills in assembling sets.

Would it be possible for you to send me a short testimonial, addressed 'To whom it may concern', naming the productions for which I worked, and outlining my contribution to the construction of the sets. It does not need to be too long – about one side of A4. Sorry to trouble you with this, but it would be a big help. (I enclose a stamped, addressed envelope.)

I hope things are going well with 'The Players'; please remember me to everyone.

With best wishes and many thanks for your time.

Yours sincerely

Offering to undertake tests

One of the advantages of courses based upon the accumulation of credit is that assessment can be organised whenever the student is ready, rather than students having to wait for the completion of the taught programme. After all, if a student already possesses the necessary knowledge and skills, it would seem sensible to undertake the assessment process, and then to move on to new work. This is much more cost effective in terms of the student's time.

It does not necessarily follow that all students start a new course with the same level of knowledge. Some students may have had previous academic or vocational experience which enables them to complete parts of the course more rapidly. One procedure to facilitate this is to submit a portfolio containing, amongst other things, a statement of the areas in which the student would be willing to take a test. This might be the normal form of assessment test for the module or unit; or alternatively, it could be a unique form of assessment designed for the particular student.

The student might assist the process, by suggesting forms of assessment, which link with the module structure, and which relate to the learning outcomes of the programme.

Structuring the portfolio

When assembling a portfolio there is a danger of including anything and everything which the student feels might conceivably be relevant. This is really the worst possible approach to portfolio preparation. It can certainly produce an impressive looking document, but it is likely to be bulky and extremely difficult for the tutor to assess.

The tutor will have to read lengthy documents and to attempt to identify the parts that are relevant to the module outcomes. This can be extremely difficult and time consuming. In addition, arguably it is not the responsibility of the tutor to identify the relevant parts of the evidence.

The best way to proceed is to identify the shortest or most succinct pieces of evidence which will satisfy the learning outcomes. The portfolio should be as short as possible, compatible with providing acceptable evidence. In this form, it will be easier to assess, and any necessary amendments can be more easily made.

Presentation

A portfolio is never an easy document to read and assess. It inevitably consists of a wide variety of documents and evidence, yet it is possible to present this material in a form which helps the assessor.

PRACTICAL ADVICE

There are a number of simple strategies which can make a portfolio easier to read. While there is no standard format, a few basic suggestions may be helpful.

1. Keep the evidence as brief as is reasonably possible;
2. Use a secure but compact file such as a lever-arch;
3. Use plastic wallets wherever possible. Documents can be placed back to back in these;
4. Use 'highlighting' pens to draw the reader's attention to important pieces of evidence;
5. Provide a clear label on each plastic wallet to indicate the section/page number and the contents;
6. Provide a key at the front, near the contents page, to indicate any coding system for the evidence. Consider using colour codes, indicated by self-adhesive coloured paper circles.

These are relatively simple measures but can make a big difference to the appearance of the portfolio. With a little bit of ingenuity, it is possible to create a reader-friendly portfolio.

The most important aspect of presentation is to compartmentalise the evidence and to relate this to the learning outcomes of the award for which the portfolio is being submitted. The portfolio should start with a title page, which states clearly the name of the award, and the sections to which the portfolio relates.

A detailed contents page should follow the title page. This should list the relevant modules of the award, along with the learning outcomes of those modules and the reference numbers (if appropriate). Each learning outcome should be accompanied by a page or section number of the portfolio at which relevant evidence can be found. The reader is thus enabled to locate the evidence for each learning outcome. It may also be the case that there is evidence in different sections of the portfolio relating to a single outcome. This should be noted in the contents page.

It also follows that on a single page of the portfolio, there may be pieces of evidence which relate to different learning outcomes. This should be cross referenced in an unambiguous fashion. The purpose is to create a portfolio which has an entirely logical and systematic structure.

Using your mentor's advice

The normal procedure on an educational or training programme is to appoint a mentor or counsellor to help the student prepare the portfolio. The mentor will not normally be allowed to take any part in the assessment procedure. The mentor's role will be restricted to providing advice.

However, the mentor is probably an experienced tutor who actually does assess the portfolios of other students. There is thus a crossing-over of roles for each individual mentor. For some students they act as mentors, while for others they act as assessors. They may even visit other institutions and act as external assessors or verifiers. In this capacity they would be evaluating the entire assessment procedure in that institution.

Inevitably then, the mentor brings a considerable amount of expertise to the counselling role. The mentor will, for example, have had access to the reports of the external assessors for that institution, and will be aware of the procedures and evidence which they see as desirable. This inevitably conditions the nature of the advice given. The mentor is likely to be able to view the portfolio from the perspective of the assessor, and this generally makes the advice more pertinent.

How will your portfolio be assessed?

It is quite common for two assessors to be involved in portfolio assessment. The reason for this is that portfolio evidence can vary widely from one student to another, and the process of making judgements can be more complex than in the case of, say, assessing an essay or research report. The assessor may need to make a series of evaluative judgements in comparing evidence with learning outcomes.

It is reassuring for assessors that they are able to consult a colleague concerning their judgements, and it is also reassuring for students that two tutors have compared their assessment of the portfolio. Such a procedure is likely to enhance the validity and reliability of the assessment. It will often be the case that an assessor who is employed externally to the institution will act in a moderating role, comparing the assessment process with that operating in similar institutions. This moderating process seeks to assure the comparability of awards between institutions.

Each internal assessor will normally complete an assessment sheet which indicates in particular the ways in which the evidence relates to the learning outcomes. If major differences exist between the assessors then some form of arbitration procedure will be instituted. The result will be an agreed grade or assessment decision.

What assessment criteria will be used?

The assessors will first seek to establish that the evidence presented is at the required academic or skill level for the award in question. An assessor will be able to ascertain quite rapidly whether, for example, an essay on economics contains the level of analysis required for a particular economics module. In most academic subjects, it may be reasonably straightforward to resolve questions of level, provided that the evidence is of an academic nature. The difficulty tends to arise where practical or vocational evidence is assembled to meet academic outcomes. For example, a portfolio may contain evidence of economic understanding derived from work in a bank or insurance company. It may be problematic to equate this with academic learning. It may be necessary to require some evidence of conceptual discussion or understanding in order to match the evidence with an academic course in economics.

Having examined questions of academic or skill level, it is essential for assessors to satisfy themselves that the evidence derives from the student in question. The assessor is concerned to know that the person named on the portfolio cover, actually wrote the economics essay.

The oral examination has an important function in this respect. It provides a forum for the assessor to establish authenticity of evidence, by, in this case, discussing economics concepts with the student. In the case of practical skills such as joinery, the assessor will have the opportunity to question the student on certain procedures, for example, fitting a new window frame. An experienced joiner may be able to tell quite quickly, through a question and answer process, whether a student understands the key stages of fitting a frame. It is clearly not the same as seeing the procedure being carried out, but is far superior to ducumentary evidence alone.

The assessors will wish to satisfy themselves that not only does the evidence match the learning outcomes, and is thus relevant and appropriate, but also that there is sufficient evidence. Although the evidence should be succinct and precise, it should also be adequate in quantity to cover all of the requirements of the outcomes.

Finally, the evidence should confirm that the learning is up to date. References and testimonials play an important part in establishing currency, but the oral examination is also relevant here.

The oral examination

Levels of some skills diminish with time. Fluency in speaking a foreign language, for example, diminishes without practice. Familiarity with particular computer software reduces when it is not used regularly. The purpose of the oral examination is to try to establish the level of currency of the knowledge or skill.

The concept of the portfolio is that the learning should be equivalent to that of an individual who has recently completed the educational programme in question. The portfolio is simply an alternative means of establishing that learning has taken place, and that the student can currently use that learning. As we have discussed, it is rarely easy to decide on the type of evidence to include in the portfolio. One of the major functions of the oral examination is to determine whether that learning has been retained and can be used in practical situations.

Summary

- Think carefully about the learning outcomes relating to the portfolio.
- Choose evidence which is relevant to the outcomes.
- Select material which covers the range of outcomes.
- Wherever possible, provide evidence of current learning.
- You can use testimonials to demonstrate that learning is current.
- Provide a detailed contents page.
- Make sure the layout of the portfolio is systematic and related to the

5

THE SEMINAR OR TUTORIAL PAPER

Seminars and tutorials differ widely in form and purpose, yet are a common feature of tertiary education. Before examining the nature of the seminar paper, it may be helpful to consider the different forms which the seminar and tutorial can take.

Perhaps the archetypal tutorial is a one-to-one meeting between student and tutor, often taking place in the tutor's study or room. The term 'group tutorial' is also used, however, to indicate a meeting involving the tutor and perhaps five or six students. The tutorial may involve a student or students preparing an essay or paper, or there may simply be a discussion around a specific topic, unsupported by any documentation. The tutorial may be led by the tutor or by a student, or there may be no leader. The purposes of the tutorial may vary enormously:

- To enable the tutor to advise the student(s) on the preparation of a piece of assessed work such as an essay or research dissertation;
- To enable the tutor and student(s) to explore further a topic which has been introduced in a lecture;
- To enable students to develop techniques of group communication and oral argument;
- To enable a student to prepare in advance a position paper on a particular issue, and then to present that argument to a group;
- To enable students to consolidate work which has been covered previously;

- To enable the tutor to provide feedback on an already assessed piece of work;
- To provide a context in which the tutor can assess a student on skills at presenting a systematic oral argument.

The word 'seminar' is used in a generally similar context to tutorial, but there are sometimes subtle differences of application. One can, for example, attend a tutorial without there being a fixed subject, but one normally speaks of attending a seminar *on* something. In other words, a seminar tends to have a more precise subject-based focus. The word can also imply a slightly larger group than a tutorial. There is certainly a sense in which one expects some kind of focused input at a seminar, whereas this need not necessarily occur at a tutorial.

There is the notion, then, that a discussion document or paper is a likely medium through which to introduce a topic at a seminar. There are no real prescriptions for the format of the seminar. There may be only one paper presented, or there may be several. The tutor may exert leadership over the group, or the group may operate totally democratically with no leader at all. The seminar may be one of a series held at regular intervals, or it may be a single, isolated event. The following could be considered the main purposes of the seminar:

- To facilitate an exchange of ideas and views on a specific topic;
- To enable a student to reflect upon an issue, and to present a reasoned paper on that issue to a group;
- To enable the tutor to teach a particular topic, using the students' seminar papers as a vehicle for the teaching.

Having established that the seminar and tutorial can exist in a variety of different forms, the remainder of this chapter will concentrate on the preparation of a student paper on a particular issue for presentation to a group. This is assumed to be the most characteristic of all the different possible formats, but much of what is said could equally be applied to the preparation of a paper for a one-to-one meeting with a tutor.

The seminar paper is designed to address a specific issue, problem or topic, but it is not an essay. The essay is an exclusively written form of communication, designed to be taken away and read slowly and carefully. The seminar paper on the other hand, is a written document designed to accompany oral discussion and debate. It may also accompany a fairly formal oral presentation. This characteristic has important consequences for the form of the seminar paper.

It should be short enough, for example, to enable the reader to absorb the arguments quickly, yet sufficiently substantial to enable other students to formulate views on the issue being discussed. The emphasis should be upon a concise structure and a succinct writing style.

Preparing background notes

The preparation and delivery of a seminar paper is a complex activity. It has much in common with teaching at any level. The paper has to be thoroughly prepared and delivered to an audience which may prove to be rather critical. The deliverer of the paper must be prepared to answer difficult questions on the topic. At the same time, the paper and the delivery of that paper must retain the interest of the other seminar members.

It is, therefore, essential for the speaker to have a wide knowledge of the subject, yet this must be condensed somehow into a fairly brief paper. The speaker must be able to respond to questions on both the paper and on peripheral, connected topics.

Background reading should commence with previous lecture notes and then extend to books and journal articles as an understanding of the topic develops. As early as possible, it is best to try to categorise the notes, in order to help information retrieval later. As new information is uncovered it is best to write it under these categories. Eventually sufficient notes will have been made, and the categories can form the basis for the structure of the actual paper.

PRACTICAL ADVICE

If, for example, you are making notes for a seminar on the early influences on a named poet, then it may be possible from an early stage, to decide on a few important categories. These might be:

- parents and the cultural life of the family
- school teachers and school activities
- friends and early attempts at writing
- poets and writers who provided guidance
- university lecturers and fellow students

Summarising evidence and argument

Just as a good teacher or lecturer should not make the delivery of a subject bewilderingly complex, the seminar paper should be to the point, and capable of retaining interest. There is normally insufficient space to provide lots of corroborating evidence and citations. The general nature of evidence should be summarised, rather than listing every single piece of data.

PRACTICAL ADVICE

Consider these two extracts, relating to the above example about the life of a poet:

> **1** Smith (1987) conducted interviews with two school friends of the poet, who indicated that early poems had been contributed to the local paper. These poems have been identified and are also recorded in the Proceedings of the local Arts Society. This early success may have motivated the poet, who implied the same in an interview many years later in the school magazine. Jones (1991) who arranged the magazine article, has also noted this suggestion in a paper in the Journal of Poetical History.
>
> **2** The poet appears to have been greatly motivated while still at school, by having poems accepted in the local paper. (Smith,1987)

The careful documentation of the first extract is more suited to a highly academic article in a scholarly journal. The style of the second extract is more suitable for a seminar paper which is intent on summarising issues and retaining the interest of the group.

Members of the seminar group can use the ideas in the paper as stimulus material, and follow up the issues in which they are interested.

Length and structure

Clearly, different tutors will suggest different lengths for seminar papers, but in general the length is much shorter than an essay or research report. If there is some flexibility over the length, then it should be determined by the planned mode of delivery. A seminar paper can be delivered in three basic ways:

1 Distributed to all seminar group members, including the tutor, a few days before the seminar, in order that it can be read carefully in advance;
2 Distributed at the start of the seminar, and referred to by group members during the talk;
3 Distributed at the end of the seminar, to be taken away and read in detail as reference material.

In the case of methods 1 and 3, a length of say 1500 words or 5 sides of A4 may be reasonable. If method 2 is used, the paper should be shorter to enable easy reference during the seminar.

The structure should relate to the main categories already determined while the background reading was being conducted. These categories can form the basis for subheadings, which help the reader to focus quickly upon the different sections of the paper.

References

A seminar paper should be written in order to be read fairly quickly. It is not necessary to employ detailed citations of the type which would normally be found in say, a research report. It may not be necessary to include actual quotations in the text. However, the principle of referencing cannot be avoided, and it is probably best to adopt a strategy which involves mentioning writers briefly. The bibliography in its conventional form can be kept fairly short. It may be possible, however, to allude to other sources in general terms, without providing detailed quotations. This demonstrates to the reader that a literature search has been undertaken, and also indicates the location where further references can be found. The writing style for this general referencing might be as follows:

Considerable work on this subject was carried out at Northern University between 1956 and 1970 (see in particular Jones, 1960). or

Articles written within this perspective are regularly published in the Journal of Proactive Research.

One or two complete references can be provided in the bibliography at the end of the paper. These can be for indicative purposes only, to enable readers to access the general literature.

Objectivity

The seminar paper should conform to all the conventions of academic writing which have been discussed previously. However, it is worth bearing in mind that it is intended to be delivered to an audience, albeit a small one, and therefore that it should stimulate discussion. There is a case for the seminar paper deliberately arguing an issue from a particular perspective in order to provoke an argument from the opposite viewpoint. If this device is adopted then it is essential to state in the paper what the chosen perspective is. This prevents any accusation of bias. It is preferable to state this in the introduction to the paper, so that the readers will immediately adjust to the framework within which the arguments are being presented. They can simultaneously think of alternative viewpoints to be proposed in the seminar. Examples of appropriate introductions for this type of approach are as follows:

It is possible to analyse the circumstances of economic aid to the developing world from a number of viewpoints. This paper will adopt a conflict perspective, exploring the interface between donor and recipient governments, and charting the implications of the large-scale movement of capital.

or

The post-war period of the twentieth century is sometimes described as if it has been dominated by a series of localised conflicts in different parts of the world. This paper will argue that the predominant characteristic of this period has been consensus, to the extent that major conflict has been avoided and significant developments have been achieved towards world peace.

In a sense, it does not matter if the argument of the seminar paper does not convince the majority of the students in the group. The writer has conceded at the beginning that a particular viewpoint is being argued, and the success of the paper rests solely upon the logic and thoroughness with which the arguments are presented.

Writing for oral presentation

The seminar paper is only part of the total presentation of a seminar. In some ways, a student presenting a paper is cast in the role of tutor for that session. It is possible, of course, simply to read out the paper to the group, and then to wait for questions to emerge. But this approach is rather unimaginative, given that the group can read the paper for themselves.

Of all the possible approaches, it is preferable to distribute the paper in advance, so that group members can read it carefully and think about the arguments. They can begin to formulate their views, and prepare things to say in the seminar. It is then necessary for the seminar presenter to give only a summary of the paper, and to remind the group of the key arguments for the particular viewpoint being advocated.

This summary can be presented in a variety of ways, but is most professionally done using an overhead projector. The acetate slides need not be written by hand but can be prepared on a computer and then photocopied on to the acetate. The main thing to remember about using overhead projectors is to keep the writing on the slide as brief and to the point as possible. The words on the slide are intended to act both as summaries of the topic, and also as prompts for the speaker. A sheet of plain paper can used to reveal each section of the slide as it is needed. This provides a structure for the talk, and prevents the deliverer of the seminar inadvertently forgetting something.

Another method of achieving the same effect is to use a flip chart. The summaries can be written on large sheets of paper before the seminar, and then the sheets turned over one by one, as each section of the subject is discussed. Large size felt-tip pens are good for this sort of presentation. Most seminar groups are fairly small, and the flip chart is perfectly adequate for this type of situation.

A useful technique at the end of a seminar delivery is to pose questions for the group to consider. Such questions might include the issue of whether the adopted perspective was the most desirable one to use. The questions could be listed on a sheet of paper, or on an acetate, or actually written on the last page of the seminar paper itself. These questions should tend to eliminate the rather awkward silence that can develop at the end of the oral delivery.

The presentation of a seminar paper is not easy and yet by using a few simple techniques, it can be made much more straightforward and definitely less stressful. Perhaps the most difficult times are at the beginning and at the end. The start of the seminar is helped by using concise flip chart summaries.

PRACTICAL ADVICE

Here is an additional strategy to move smoothly into a group discussion at the end of a seminar.

At the beginning of the seminar, before you start your introduction, say something such as the following:

> This brief talk will provide a summary of the paper which you have all received. I hope to keep the talk to about ten minutes to allow for discussion afterwards. When I have gone through the main points of the paper, I would like to go round the group and ask everyone in turn to make a few brief comments about the issues raised. We can then have a fuller general discussion.

This strategy should ensure that all group members listen to you carefully in order to plan what they are going to say. In addition, it has the advantage that at the end of your talk, it immediately moves the focus from you to the rest of the group.

Preparing supplementary arguments

The seminar is very much a group activity. It does not depend solely upon the deliverer of the paper. If group members do not contribute, then the seminar is not going to be a success. It is, therefore, a good idea for all members to consider their own position with regard to the issues raised in the seminar paper. These arguments can be written down in brief, as a preparation for the discussion. It is far better to do this, than to find that no ideas come to mind during the discussion.

Think of alternative viewpoints and arguments to propose, in advance of the seminar, whether or not you have the responsibility of delivering the paper.

– How will your paper be assessed? –

It is perhaps less common for a true seminar paper to be formally assessed, than with many other types of assignment such as essays. The main reason for this is that the seminar paper is fairly short, and that it can be difficult to separate the paper from the success of the delivery process and the ensuing discussion. It may be more common for the tutor to provide oral and/or written feedback on the process. In some cases, however, tutors ask students to prepare an essay rather than a shorter paper for a seminar, so the essay may be assessed in the normal manner.

The tutor may wish to assess the seminar paper formally, and the normal practice may be to provide an overall assessment of the paper along with the delivery.

What criteria will be used?

As seminars and seminar papers differ somewhat in format, there may be a range of criteria which tutors employ in assessment. Many of the following are likely to be used:

- the extent to which the seminar paper is written in a lucid style, and the arguments are presented with precision
- the degree to which the paper covers the main issues involved in the subject
- extent and appropriateness of the bibliography
- clarity of the presentation
- use of appropriate visual aids
- the extent to which the group was involved in the delivery
- facilitation of the ensuing discussion

Summary

- Prepare background notes by categorising the subject.
- Write the paper as concisely as possible.
- Summarise evidence wherever possible.
- Distribute the paper in advance of the seminar.
- Prepare visual support material for the talk.
- Restrict visual aids to subheadings and summaries.
- Develop strategies to involve the whole group.

6

A PLAN FOR A PROJECT OR RESEARCH STUDY

The term 'project' is a good example of a word which has acquired a variety of subtly different meanings depending upon the context. It can be used in high school, for example, to indicate a short study of a particular topic using only secondary source material. It may also be used to signify a more complex, empirical investigation which involves the collection of primary data. Finally, the word may be used in conjunction with 'research' to indicate a wide ranging and advanced investigation which may legitimately be described as a 'research project'. This use is normally reserved for research in a university context or for advanced investigations in an industrial or business context.

The terms project and research study are also used for types of assignment which lie between the examples mentioned above. In this chapter and the next, the terms project and research study will be used interchangeably to indicate the type of systematic enquiry typical of the final two years of secondary education and the first year or two of tertiary education. This type of enquiry is typically, although not exclusively, characterised as follows:

- length of between 2000 and 5000 words
- brief review of relevant secondary sources
- collection of some primary data
- clearly understood procedure for analysing the data
- appreciation of basic methods of summarising quantitative data

- ability to write clearly and logically
- capacity to draw rational conclusions based upon the data
- appropriate bibliography

Definition of research

The term 'research' tends to conjure up in our minds the idea of a complex scientific investigation in a laboratory or perhaps of someone translating ancient texts in a museum library. The popular image of research seems to be that it is: extremely advanced; conducted by clever people; on esoteric subjects; only for the initiated; impossible to understand for the non-academic; published in obscure, scholarly journals. If this is so, then there seems to be a need for some public relations work!

It is perfectly true that some research is complex, and that it would be difficult for the layperson to understand. However, it still should be possible to explain the essence of the research in fairly straightforward terms. Quite often, research seems complicated because of the technical terms used. If simpler, everyday words are used instead, then the research appears much less complex. It should be possible to explore the basic characteristics of research, which are true for all kinds of investigations in different subject areas. Perhaps first, we can list some different examples of research activities, and then analyse the fundamental characteristics which they share.

Some examples of research might be:

- The attempt to synthesise in the laboratory, a chemical which occurs naturally in plants;
- The investigation of the source of some damaging vibration in a large turbine;
- An enquiry into the main causes of motorway accidents;
- An investigation into the strategies used by young children when learning to read;
- Research into the voting habits at general elections of a particular occupational group.

The above are examples of research investigations from chemistry, engineering, transport studies, educational psychology and social science. Perhaps the most obvious feature is that they are all seeking to discover something new, or to investigate something which is not known or understood. Research involves trying to resolve problems or at least trying to understand them a little better.

We would also expect all of these topics to be investigated in a fairly logical way. In the final example concerning voting habits we would not expect the researcher simply to interview the first few people available, but rather to have a systematic interviewing strategy. When investigating motorway accidents we would be surprised if the researcher came to a conclusion after investigating only one or two accidents. There is an expectation that research activity should proceed carefully and thoughtfully, should have a clear system for amassing information and for analysing it. Research is, therefore, systematic and logical.

It is also important that research is public, in the sense that the procedures and results are available for inspection. If someone claims one day to have discovered a wonder drug, the first thing we would want to know is how it was made and how it is known to be a wonder drug. If the experimental results were not forthcoming, we would be reluctant to term this medical research. For an activity to be research, it must be available for scrutiny by other researchers and scientists, in order that they can check the results and, if necessary, try to replicate the research.

The public accountability of research is important. This is really the significance of researchers seeking to publish their results and findings in scholarly journals. It is not merely publishing and seeing their work in print which is important. Far more crucial is the act of placing their work in the public domain and before the scrutiny of fellow researchers.

These then are the main characteristics of research, and perhaps it is worth summarising them briefly. Research involves:

- the investigation of a new problem or issue
- a systematic and logical process of investigation
- the public dissemination of results

Research can involve much more than these three fundamental characteristics. A frequent function of research is to generate theories about the world. Theories are general statements which both describe the nature of events and which can also be used to predict future occurrences. Theories can be generated in the social sciences just as much as in the natural sciences such as physics and chemistry.

We are probably more familiar with the word applied to examples such as the 'Theory of Gravity'. This theory *describes* what happens when we let go of an object which we are holding; and it also *predicts* what will happen in future similar cases. However, it seeks to do more than that. In addition, it provides an *explanation* for the phenomenon of objects falling to earth. The same characteristics of description, prediction, and explanation apply to research and theory construction in the social sciences.

Suppose someone is researching football hooliganism. The first stage would probably be to observe instances of such behaviour, and to describe the main features. These might include aspects such as the positioning of spectators; the degree of supervision of the crowd; access to alcohol. From a series of careful descriptions of examples of football hooliganism, it might be possible to begin to understand some of the causes and to provide a provisional explanation. It may, therefore, be possible to predict situations in which hooliganism would be more likely to occur again. A theory of football hooliganism could be constructed, which would include elements of explanation and prediction, both based firmly upon accurate description.

It is still possible, however, to conduct a serious enquiry and to leave it at the level of description. It can still legitimately be termed research, even though there is little prediction and explanation. This view of research removes it from the realms of 'the ivory tower' and places it firmly within the grasp of anyone who is willing to meet the fundamental requirements of addressing a new topic, being systematic, and reporting the results. There is an enormous and important role for accurate, descriptive research. This is particularly important in the social sciences, where the wide diversity of human behaviour is difficult to examine systematically without a firm basis in observational data.

One of the fundamental arguments of this chapter is that this perception of research encourages people to take part in systematic enquiry, because it is seen to be possible to make significant advances in knowledge by simple, straightforward techniques. Research ceases to be a complex, esoteric activity, and becomes the province of all, if there is a willingness to follow a few basic, commonsense methods.

Planning

The systematic nature of research makes it important to have a plan of action. This is not simply a matter of listing quickly the various things that a researcher plans to do. Research is a serious activity, perhaps particularly when people are involved as the subjects, and it is essential to try to look ahead and to anticipate the effects upon the research subjects.

Perhaps we can take as an example the issues inherent in educational research. Suppose that a researcher wishes to interview some schoolchildren about the occupations in which they are interested. This may seem at first sight to be totally innocuous, and to have no hidden difficulties or problems. However, during interviews children may start to talk about the jobs which their parents have, and may indeed begin to discuss matters which parents might feel should be confidential to the family. Children might go home and say that they have been interviewed 'about their parents' jobs'. This might, of course, cause some difficulty for the school. In a case such as this, the school would almost certainly contact parents, prior to any research, in order to clarify the exact nature of the activity. The need for a careful plan is clear. In research and data collection involving human beings there is considerable scope for misunderstanding, and one of the best ways to minimise this is to think out carefully a plan for the research project which takes careful account of activities which could conceivably cause discomfort to respondents. These sorts of issues are in the province of 'research ethics' – an increasingly important aspect of research.

Within research ethics, one of the central principles is that of 'informed consent'. This is the principle that when people are asked to take part in a research project and to provide data, they should be given full information about the research and should have total freedom to opt out of the project if they have reservations about it. As part of the research plan it is important to consider how the project will be explained to potential respondents in order to comply with the principle of informed consent.

If all of the aspects of a research project are not explained to potential respondents, this could be viewed as an infrigement of privacy, especially if they are asked to discuss their own attitudes towards an issue.

PRACTICAL ADVICE

It is a good idea to have a standard text ready to either read out to potential respondents or to give them to read. Try to phrase this carefully, making sure that you do not miss out anything important. As an example, suppose that you are collecting oral history data on everyday life in England during the Second World War, and that you hope to interview neighbours and friends of the family. You might prepare a handout which says something like this:

EVERYDAY LIFE IN ENGLAND DURING THE SECOND WORLD WAR

> I am doing a research project for my history course at college, and would appreciate your help. I am trying to collect information on everyday aspects of life during the Second World War. Anything which you remember will help me to build up a picture of what things were like.
>
> Would you be willing for me to interview you for about fifteen minutes? When I write up my project I will not mention your name. If you agree, I would like to tape record the interview, but if you are unhappy about this, then I will just write down notes. The tape recording or notes will be destroyed when I have written up my project.
>
> If you would prefer not to be interviewed, but can provide me with other kinds of information, then I would be delighted to receive this. You might have old documents, for example, which you would be willing to let me see.
>
> I would be happy to let you have a summary of the project when it is completed. Please fill in the reply slip below if you would like to help. Thank you.

The reply slip can include several possible dates and times for an interview, and the respondent asked to tick the one most appropriate or convenient.

Another aspect of research ethics and one which can be thought out clearly in the research plan, is the issue of reporting the names of people and institutions in the published research. It is wise to give some early thought to this, since it might affect advice given to respondents.

Individuals have a right to privacy, and even though they may offer to help with a research project, that does not necessarily mean that they are willing to have their names quoted in a final report. In any case, the use of the actual names of respondents in a report, imposes certain practical responsibilities and pressures on the researcher. In such cases, it would really be necessary to allow the named respondents to read through and check anything that was printed in their name. The most usual procedure in research reports is to use fictional names for respondents, although it is also possible to refer to them as 'Respondent A', 'Respondent B' and so on. It is a good idea to consider issues such as fictional names during the preparation of the research plan. Having thought out a policy on this, it can be discussed with respondents in order to obtain their agreement in principle.

PRACTICAL ADVICE

When you have chosen your respondents, and assuming that they agree to the use of fictional names, it is important to keep a checklist which relates real names to fictional names. You will probably always think of respondents in terms of their real names, and an effort may be needed to transpose real to fictional names in the research account.

Keep a checklist in a secure place as an *aide-mémoire* while carrying out and writing up the research, and then destroy it when the research report is completed. This is probably the closest that you can get to ensuring confidentiality.

It is also worth noting the importance of maintaining the anonymity of institutions. Not only is this important as institutions are becoming increasingly conscious of what may be written about them, but also because naming of an institution can cause an individual to be identified. If someone is described as the holder of a specific post at a named institution, then this can be tantamount to identifying the person.

It has almost become the norm in research reports to employ a fictional name for an institution.

Writing a precise title

This might seem to be one of the easiest aspects of a research plan, but in fact it can often be quite difficult. In a sense, the title determines the entire context and framework of the proposed research. The title should not claim that the research is of a particular type when this is not evident from the subsequent report. For example, in the case of the following title:

A survey of insurance companies concerning their response to recent government legislation

Research based upon this title, must clearly involve the collection of data from a reasonably large number of insurance companies. Without this approach, it can hardly claim to be a survey. To take another example:

A comparison of primary education in England and Australia

The key word here is 'comparison'. If there is no intention of being able to draw a legitimate comparison, then this word should not be used in the title. Its use implies that there is an equivalent amount of data available from the two countries. If, for example, the primary data is from one country and only secondary data is available from the other, then arguably the research is not going to result in a genuine comparison, and the word 'comparison' should not be used.

Titles then, are a commitment to conducting the research in a certain manner. Think carefully when constructing a precise title. It is also helpful if the title is not too long and rambling. There can be a temptation to construct a lengthy title on the grounds that it helps the researcher to describe the nature of the research more exactly. The result, however, can often be cumbersome:

An investigation of the extent to which women have risen to management posts in a large organisation based upon a case-study approach using interviews and participant observation

The length of this title actually begins to obscure the subject matter of the research plan. Far better to say simply:

A case study investigation of women in management

or

Women in management: a case study approach

There are sufficient key words in this abbreviated title to attract the reader who has an interest in the general area. A glance through the introduction will then inform the reader whether it will be of interest to read the study further.

Describing the problem

Once the title to a research plan has been clarified, it is usual to describe the broad themes and context of the proposed research in an introductory section. The purpose of this section is to introduce the reader rapidly to the main research issue, so that the remainder of the research plan is easily understandable afterwards. The introduction should cover some or all of the following issues:

- the nature of the research problem which is to be investigated;
- the way in which the problem arose or came to the attention of the researcher;
- a brief mention of previous, related research;
- the proposed location for the research;
- a description of the context of the data collection;
- the significance of the research project in a wider context;
- the possible application of the research.

All of these issues should be dealt with in a fairly broad manner, as further details will generally be provided later in the research plan. The purpose of the introduction is to provide an overview of the plan in order to set the scene for the reader.

One of the most important aspects of the introduction is that it explains any matters of particular interest concerning the context of the proposed research. If, for example, someone anticipates collecting data in the organisation in which they work, and intends to interview some of the people with whom they work, then this is a significant aspect of the research context.

It is important to describe the role of the researcher in the organisation, since this may affect the interview process with colleagues. Relative status within an organisation can have a considerable effect upon discourse between two people. In addition, the fact that someone is researching within their own workplace means they can overlook certain things simply because he or she is familiar with the setting. An external researcher may attach significance to different data, simply because of the unfamiliarity of the environment.

The title and the introductory section are the first two parts of the plan to be read, and as such should help the reader to focus quickly upon the nature and purpose of the research plan. The rest of the plan should, as far as possible, follow a systematic structure.

Writing within an accepted structure

PRACTICAL ADVICE

Write the research plan so that a reader unfamiliar with the topic would be able to follow the research strategy without any further information.

The above may seem rather strange advice, when in all probability no-one else is going to use the plan. However, it does provide a good test of its practicality. If, at one stage in the plan, it is not clear exactly how the data collection will proceed, then this should be specified. A good plan is unambiguous, and can be followed systematically from beginning to end, with a minimum of uncertainty.

This is not always easy to achieve, since it can be quite difficult to project ahead and to anticipate all of the potential difficulties which can arise. One of the safest ways to proceed is to adhere to a commonly accepted structure for a research plan, as this helps to minimise the risk of overlooking something important. It is no guarantee, of course, but the structure acts as a kind of *aide-mémoire* with regard to the crucial aspects of the plan.

The following are the main sub-sections which can be used for a research plan:

- title
- introduction and context
- aims
- review of previous research in the area
- proposed data collection methods
- data analysis
- data presentation
- bibliography

This list is not exhaustive, and should not be regarded as an absolute. However, it does represent the general pattern of research plans, and should provide a structure to cope with most kinds of research projects.

Aims

The aims of a research study are the general goals of that study – the issues which hopefully will be investigated and clarified by the end of the research. It is important to think these out clearly before the research commences. In a sense, the entire research project is constructed around the aims. Once the aims are established, the researcher will probably consult them over and over again, to ensure that the investigation is staying on target, and is indeed enquiring into the very issues which were intended to be investigated.

The aims of a project also assume considerable importance towards the end of a study when all of the data has been collected and analysed, and the conclusion is being written. It is at this point that the researcher should revisit the aims, and try to ensure that they are addressed one by one in the conclusion. It may be that not all of the aims have been met, and this is often inevitable. The conclusion of a project should, however, examine each of the aims individually and review the extent to which that aim has been met. Reasons should be given for any failure to meet the stated aims.

In the light of this, it is probably a good idea to be fairly circumspect when writing aims, and to try to be neither too modest nor too ambitious. A set of aims for a project should perhaps display the following characteristics. They should:

- cover the realistic goals for the investigation.
- be expressed in a clear and concise manner.
- be capable of being measured (one should know how to judge whether they have been achieved)

As an example we can try to develop a set of aims for a hypothetical research investigation. Let us imagine that this is a study of the extent of corrosion by natural, spring water on domestic copper piping. In some parts of the country, houses use natural supplies of water, which is pumped into the house and then circulates as a normal system. However, such water can be acidic and corrode the copper piping resulting in inconvenience through sporadic leaks. In a study to investigate this phenomenon and to make recommendations for improvements, the following could be a range of suitable aims:

1 To investigate the pH levels of a variety of spring water sources;
2 To conduct laboratory-based investigations of the rates of corrosion of standard copper piping by different samples of water;
3 To investigate the possible relationship between corrosion rate and the variables of pH and temperature;
4 To carry out case studies of houses using spring water sources.

It is probably best to enumerate aims, as in this example. It will be easier then to refer to them in later sections of the research report, and it is perhaps easier for the reader to understand what the research enquiry is setting out to achieve.

Review of previous investigation in the area

It is perhaps a popular misconception of research that it is the province of the great intellect making huge strides into uncharted territory, and making a single, enormous contribution to knowledge. No doubt there have been some cases of this in the history of human enquiry, but much more typical is that research consists of a gradual, incremental process where small additions are made to existing understanding and knowledge.

A research project is rather like a small building block which is balanced precariously upon many other building blocks put there by previous researchers. The purpose of this section is to explore the nature of this previous work and of its relationship with the proposed project. Ideally, the sources which are referenced should be research studies themselves, perhaps obtained from journals. However, for many research projects it is difficult to locate studies which are closely-related, and frequently a compromise has to be made by using references which are less precisely related.

The normal manner in which this section of a research plan is written, is to name the author and date of publication of each work in turn, and in each case to write a synopsis of perhaps 100 or so words summarising the study. Let us suppose that the research plan concerns a historical study of the life of a modern writer. The 'review of the previous literature' section might well begin in the following way:

> LITERATURE REVIEW
>
> The source materials on the life of this widely read novelist can be divided into three main categories:
>
> **1** Critical and biographical studies.
> **2** Public documents eg. school records from the period when he was a school-teacher.
> **3** Private papers such as diaries and correspondence, which are part of the writer's estate.
>
> Source materials will be discussed under these three main headings.
>
> <u>Critical and Biographical Studies</u>
>
> The first main study was that of Smith (1961) who provides a short analysis of the first five novels and the only volume of poetry which was published. The book concentrates however on detailing the early life of the writer, including his days as a student in London, and the first few years as a teacher. There are some early photographs although these have become well known through publication in later studies. The most interesting and revealing data is on the last few years of school, prior to going to university, and the account of the many discussions held with his English teacher at school. This is a valuable book, but subsequent research has enabled later books to provide a richer picture of the life.
>
> An example of this greater detail is provided in Jones (1969) . . . .

The length of this section will be determined by the length of the research plan, but it should be adequate to illustrate the previous work in the field. Rather than trying to write this section all at once, it may be easier to collect the information gradually while background reading is carried out.

PRACTICAL ADVICE

Whenever you read a book or journal article which might be relevant to a future project or research study, write a brief summary of the book in a section of your file which you keep for that purpose. Make sure that you also note down the key bibliographic details which are:

- author surname and initials
- title
- date of publication
- place of publication
- publisher
- page numbers (in the case of a journal article or book chapter)
- the ISBN number
- where you saw the book

If you build up a large number of these kinds of summaries in the areas in which you are interested, then it will help enormously when you are compiling reviews of literature. It is important, though, to keep your notes up to date, and to keep reading the latest published works.

One way of recording information about books which may be useful in the future is to list the chapter titles.

The full bibliographic details of the books or articles mentioned are not given in the main text, but recorded in the Bibliography or References section at the end of the research plan. The different ways of setting this out are discussed in detail in Chapter 8.

Proposed data collection methods

The purpose of this section is to explain the method by which it is planned to collect data, and also to explain and justify the strategy which is selected. Generally, it is preferable to avoid the approach of describing all possible or potential research methods, and then selecting one for the particular study. In order to write such a section properly, the account would be too long. It is probably better to say simply that a particular data collection procedure has been chosen, and then to give brief reasons for conducting the research in this way.

It is worth remembering that this is a research 'plan' and not an essay on research methodology. It is best to be as succinct as possible, while at the same time providing a brief justification for the decisions made. It may be helpful to consider a practical example.

Suppose that it is planned to investigate the way in which prospective new staff are interviewed for jobs in a large organisation. The researcher may well be prohibited by the personnel department from seeing any application forms or personnel records, but may be given permission to approach present staff about their appointment process and also managers about their perception of the appointment interview. In a case such as this, the data collection section may begin something as follows:

> Data Collection Method
>
> The staff appointment procedure is a sensitive issue. It is not unknown for unsuccessful candidates to either ask for reasons why they were not successful, or to actually appeal against the decision. Managers tend to document the process carefully, and keep detailed records. Preliminary enquiries suggested that both managers and staff would be reluctant to complete questionnaires on the subject. The vast majority approached also stated that tape-recorded interviews would be unacceptable. There was however, an indication that some people would be prepared to take part in an interview if total anonymity was assured, and if they had the freedom not to respond to unacceptable questions.
>
> The intention is therefore to employ structured interviews based on a preplanned schedule of closed questions. This will ensure that the responses to a particular question are of a fairly uniform type, and can be readily analysed when all data has been collected. The data collection method is, in effect, a variant of the questionnaire, with the questions being put orally, and the responses written down immediately by the researcher.

> For the staff interviews, a random sample of sixty staff will be selected from the staff lists. Interviews will be conducted with as many respondents as are willing to participate.

The style of writing should be clear and straightforward. It should be capable of providing clear instructions to someone else. This can be important, particularly in cases where a number of people are going to collaborate on a research investigation, and each has to understand the research plan clearly.

Data analysis methods

This section provides a summary of the planned methods for analysing the data. In a plan, it may not always be possible to predict the exact form of the data, and therefore the precise manner in which it will be analysed. However, it is better to have a planned strategy rather than none at all.

In the previous example, some of the interview schedule questions might be:

1. How many people were on the interview panel for your job?
2. How many of the panel were women?
3. Did the panel do or say anything specifically to help you feel at ease?
4. What kind of questions were asked?

Questions 1 and 2 lend themselves to a treatment different from the last two questions. It would be possible for the first two questions to add up all the responses and then to express the results numerically. In question 1 it would be easy to calculate the mean size of an interview panel; and in question 2 it would be possible to calculate the overall gender percentage figure for the interview panels.

Question 3 is less precise, in that much depends upon the opinions of the interviewees as to whether anything was done to make them feel at ease. The responses here may not fall into neat categories, and it may be necessary to create categories for the data.

In question 4 each respondent will probably remember only a few of the questions. In the case of some common questions, these will fall naturally into a single category. Other questions may well differ from interview panel to interview panel, and from interviewee to interviewee. In this case, a variety of categories will be required to encompass the different questions.

Questions 3 and 4 are examples of instances where the researcher will 'post-code' the data. This is a technique where the data is collected in such a way that it is not already grouped into categories. In post-coding, the categories have to be created once the data is collected, and the researcher has had time to examine it.

In 4 above, some of the questions might have been:

- How does your previous experience equip you for this job?
- Can you describe any staff management experience which you have had?
- Have you ever had to plan staff work rotas?
- What kind of post would you like to have in five years' time?

The first three questions are all concerned with previous experience, and would thus lend themselves to being included in the same category. The final question is different, because it projects into the future. There could, thus, be a different category for this type of question. Once the categories are established, the number of questions in each category can be determined and the results presented as a histogram, for example.

Data presentation methods

The forms of data presentation will be largely determined by the nature of the analysis itself. One general point is worth bearing in mind, however. There are some types of data which are extremely voluminous, and which it is better not to use in full. Perhaps the best example of this is interview data. Even a fairly short interview can cover many pages once it is transcribed, and it is unlikely that anything approaching all of the data will be used to draw conclusions for the research. It is certainly unnecessary to include all of the transcripts in the research report, even as an appendix.

The aim of data presentation should be to analyse a sufficient quantity of the available data, and to present the conclusions in such a way that they can be understood by the reader, without the need to read large amounts of material. The intention should be to find ways of summarising data, rather than presenting it in total.

Bibliography

The research plan need only contain an indicative bibliography. It should cite the following categories of work:

- books and journal articles quoted in the review of the literature
- several key works on the selected area of methodology
- any unpublished dissertations in the specific area

The bibliography in the actual research report will normally be longer than that of the plan, and at this stage it is necessary to include only a basic list.

Conveying ideas succinctly and accurately

A research plan need not be a long document. It is designed to summarise an intended piece of research, and also to provide instructions for the researcher or researchers. The language should be concise, impartial, and should convey ideas with clarity.

Apart from the style of writing, the choice of vocabulary for research plans can sometimes cause difficulty for students. Let us examine a few words which are commonly used:

'facts'

This word tends to be used in a sentence such as: *'The facts collected on the questionnaires will be analysed by computer.'* The difficulty with the word 'fact' is that it conveys the impression of an indisputable truth. Whenever we are examining empirical evidence, it is unlikely that we are going to come across 'facts' in this sense. We may collect evidence or data which we feel reflects the truth closely, but the small amount of doubt which remains makes it far better to avoid the word 'fact'.

Wherever there is a tendency to use 'fact' or 'facts', then 'data' will nearly always be a preferable alternative. This reflects a view of research as being to some extent a relative activity, rather than producing absolute knowledge.

'truth' or 'true'

This word might be found in the following kind of sentence: *'The evidence collected in the experiment demonstrated that the theory is true.'* The argument in the section on 'facts' tends to suggest why the word 'true' is also best avoided in a research plan. A theory may be excellent at predicting experimental results, but we can never quite be certain that one more result may be not quite as predicted. A theory is only as good as the last result. It is much better to say that a theory is 'supported' by the evidence.

Much the same applies in the case of the word 'prove' or 'proven'. A theory is not 'proved'. Similarly, a hypothesis is not 'proved'. The best word to use is 'supported.'

'qualitative and quantitative'

These words are normally understood well, but can easily be transposed or mistyped because of their similarity. Qualitative data includes all types of data which consists largely of spoken or written words. Examples include interview data, observational data, participant observation studies, and audio or video recordings.

Quantitative data includes all data which is either numerical or will be analysed in a numerical or statistical manner. Examples include physical measurements and many types of survey and questionnaire data.

Sometimes there is an overlap between the approaches. A questionnaire can include some questions which are open-ended and may be treated as qualitative data, while other questions may be 'closed' and offer discrete, quantifiable responses for statistical analysis. In such cases it may be better to avoid referring to the questionnaire as either qualitative or quantitative.

It should also be remembered that these terms do not describe specific methodologies. Rather, they are general terms which include many specific research methodologies. It is better, therefore, not to employ them in the following kind of sentence: *'The data from this research will be analysed qualitatively to produce the results.'* 'Qualitatively' in this sense has no specific meaning. The sentence should be supplemented with an explanation of the exact nature of the data, and the manner of analysis. For example, data from a sociological study which was ethnomethodological in nature, would be analysed in one way, while interview data from a management study would be analysed in another way. They would both be qualitative studies, but only in terms of the general nature of the data.

'cause'

There is a great temptation in research writing to suggest that one event may *cause* another event. The word could be used inappropriately, as in the following sentence: *'The hypothesis for this study is that reduced class size in secondary schools causes improved educational attainment.'* Causality is difficult to demonstrate in the physical sciences, but is even more so in the social sciences. There are so many different variables involved in a study of school attainment that to suggest one variable directly causes a change in another, is very difficult to demonstrate. It is far better to avoid the word 'cause', and to revise the sentence as follows: *'The hypothesis for this study is that class size is a significant factor in the educational attainment of secondary school pupils.'*

'random sample'

A random sample is a statistical device to ensure that the data collected in a research project is typical (as far as possible) of the larger population which is the subject of the research. In a random sample, every object or person in the research population has an equal opportunity of being selected. When this is the case, the researcher has more certainty of being able to generalise from the sample to the population as a whole.

The random sample, however, has no real significance or usefulness outside the notion of a statistical study. It is better to avoid the concept in other kinds of research, and also where the population is so small that a random sample has little meaning.

'researcher/respondent' and 'interviewer/interviewee'

These are useful terms to employ when discussing the collection of data. The word 'respondent' is a fairly general term for a person who provides data of some kind. The 'interviewee' is fairly self-evidently the person who responds in an interview. The only danger from a stylistic point of view is that the terms can be over-used and sound rather repetitive.

'perspective'

This is a useful word to employ in research plans, but it has subtly different meanings which depend upon the context. For example: *'The data analysis will be carried out within a functionalist perspective.'* In this sense, the word perspective means a 'conceptual framework'. It indicates that the data will be analysed using a set of interrelated concepts, which together encompass a particular view of the world. Possible synonyms are 'paradigm' or 'methodological approach.'

The word 'perspective' can also be employed in a much more general sense, approaching the use in everyday, non-academic language. For example: *'The researcher's general perspective is that enquiries of this sort should be of benefit to people, and particularly to the respondents who have provided data.'* In this sense, the word is synonymous with 'viewpoint' or 'attitude'.

— How will your plan be assessed? —

The criteria which might typically be used to assess a research plan include:

- the precision and logic of the plan
- the relevance of the research methodology
- the viability of the plan
- the applicability of the research

The plan should be straightforward and easy to understand. It should have a systematic structure which provides a guide for the researcher to progress steadily through the research project. The title and aims of the plan should lead logically to the choice of research methodology. This should be appropriate to the problem being investigated and there should be an awareness of any potential procedural difficulties in the collection of data.

The plan should be viable: that is, it should be capable of being carried out by the person who is likely to conduct the research. Plans may be impracticable because the respondents live too far away from the researcher for easy access, or because the plan is too complex for the amount of time available. There may be many other reasons which would make a plan difficult to implement. A research plan should not only be sound methodologically, but should be realistic.

In a perfect world, research should not only be of academic interest, but should also be useful. Arguably, a good research plan should propose to investigate an area where the possible results may be of practical use. There certainly could be other criteria by which to judge a research plan, but these are probably of general application. It is perhaps true to say however, that as a student assignment more attention is often given to the research report than to the research plan.

Summary

- Research involves the investigation of an issue in a systematic way, and the public dissemination of the results.
- Preparing a plan may help you in the clarification of ethical issues.
- Try to use a standard letter or approach for potential respondents.
- Use fictional names where appropriate.
- Think of a precise title.
- Write realistic aims.
- Use research terms carefully.

7

THE PROJECT OR RESEARCH REPORT

There is a range of terms used to describe a report of an academic enquiry. Apart from project and research report, there are the terms 'dissertation' and 'thesis'. It may be helpful to explain briefly the use of the latter two terms, and then to leave them out of the discussion as they normally relate to a fairly specialist context.

The terms dissertation and thesis can be and are used as synonyms, for a long and detailed academic research study, which is normally submitted to a university as a part requirement for a degree or Doctorate. It would not be too inaccurate to describe a dissertation as a long version of a research report. The dissertation would be written with the same general sections, including a review of the literature, a discussion of data collection and analysis, and then a conclusion. The difference is that the entire research methodology is much more detailed.

The research design is complex, and there is normally a detailed discussion of theoretical issues concerning methodology. The data collection procedures are likely to be sophisticated, and there will normally be an extensive amount of data to be analysed. The other important aspect of a research dissertation at Doctorate level is that it is normally expected to make a significant contribution to knowledge in the particular field.

The importance attached to methodological issues in a dissertation creates problems and issues in the writing, which are better treated separately. The remainder of this chapter will, therefore, concentrate on briefer records of research enquiries.

For whom are research reports intended?

The advice in this book is intended mainly for an academic context, assuming that reports or projects are being submitted as coursework assignments. However, it is probably worth noting in passing that reports may also be submitted to organisations outside the college or university, particularly where data has been collected in that organisation.

It is often the case that when an organisation agrees to take part in a study, and to volunteer data, that there is a request to receive a copy of the final report. There is usually little difficulty with this, as long as the anonymity of respondents is strictly preserved.

PRACTICAL ADVICE

If you intend to release a copy of the final report to an organisation from which respondents are drawn, make it clear to the respondents that this will happen. Ideally, explain this to them before you collect data. This could be seen as being part of the principle of 'informed consent'. If respondents are forewarned they may have useful suggestions to make about ways of preserving anonymity.

A variation on this issue of confidentiality occurs where data is collected from a number of different commercial or industrial organisations. Suppose that the data collected included information on the level or type of technology currently being used by an organisation. In such a case, it might be possible to guess the identity of the company in the final report, even though the names of organisations are not mentioned. Competitor companies might be able to make a shrewd guess at identity, based upon their existing knowledge of other companies. In the case of the use of technology, organisations would almost certainly wish to be careful about the disclosure of such information.

A useful way of getting round the problem is to produce an 'Executive Summary' of the report. This is a summary of the aims, research procedure and main findings. In terms of dissemination, it has a number of advantages:

1 The details of the data can be omitted, and this tends to minimise difficulties associated with confidentiality;
2 It is easier to duplicate and post, so can be sent to more people;
3 The presentation of the findings as a summary, possibly results in more people actually reading about the research.

The practice of distributing research findings is a good one, but it should be distinguished from the possibility of 'submitting' a research report to either respondents or those who may have commissioned the research, for a form of vetting prior to dissemination. The researcher should be absolutely responsible for the conduct of a research project, and for the subsequent publication of findings. It is generally undesirable that others seek to comment upon or amend a report before the researcher is satisfied that it is in its finished form. This is, of course, quite different from the situation where the researcher specifically requests help from a colleague.

Writing for your audience

A research report is not, as we might suppose, a completely objective piece of work. The analysis of data, for example, should be as objective as possible, but there are a number of parts of a report which reflect the interests, knowledge and value judgements of the writer. It is in such sections that there is scope for flexibility, and for the writer to demonstrate special skills and knowledge.

The approach taken depends on the intended destination of the report. For example, one issue which confronts all writers is that of the amount of knowledge to assume in the reader. Suppose a report is to be distributed outside an academic institution among non-specialists in the particular subject area, then a non-technical writing style is obviously required. Particular attention should be paid to the use of acronyms and other abbreviations.

PRACTICAL ADVICE

If you are using acronyms in the report, it is useful to do two things to help your readers:

1. Include a Glossary of acronyms, perhaps just after the Contents page;
2. When you use a term for the first time, write it in full, with the acronym in brackets afterwards: from then on, it will be sufficient to use the acronym alone.

It is also important to judge the amount of technical language used in the report carefully. If the research report is for the purpose of a standard academic assignment then it may be desirable to demonstrate as much awareness of technical vocabulary as possible. On the other hand, this will be less necessary if it is to be read by a non-specialist audience.

PRACTICAL ADVICE

Consider including a glossary of specialist terms at the end of the report, just before the bibliography. The glossary will consist of short definitions of the terms. It is a matter of judgement which terms to include. To define rather obvious and commonly understood terms would not be helpful. The choice of terms to define depends upon an assessment of the projected readership of the report.

Another important area is the review of the literature and the accompanying bibliography. It is advisable to select books and articles which are at the appropriate level for the research report. In the case of a pre-university project, for example, it might be possible to locate complex research papers, but these may seem inappropriate for a study at this level. Generally speaking, works selected for review and referencing should be:

- relevant to the project topic
- at an appropriate level of sophistication
- from sources normally accessed at that academic level

Getting the title right

It is tempting when preparing a title for a project, to include as many aspects of the research as possible in order to make the title as precise as possible. Normally, however, this only results in a long and cumbersome title. For example: *A study of the introduction of a programme of work-based learning and job shadowing to two groups of GCSE pupils in an inner city comprehensive school*. In some ways, the length of title is a matter of preference, but this title does seem rather too detailed and long. It could be replaced by: *A study of work-based learning in a comprehensive school*.

This short title conveys the essence of what is being investigated, and would attract the attention of someone interested in the topic.

Further details of the project, such as the nature of the sample and the location of the particular school, could easily be included in the introductory section of the report. Arguably, this would be a better approach. A good title should ideally include the key words of the project in as succinct a statement as possible.

Writing to the structure

The structure of a research report can be based upon that for a research plan outlined in Chapter 6. These headings are only for guidance. It is worth emphasising that while there are no standard headings for the sections of a research report, there is a generally accepted sequence for presenting the contents of the report. Look briefly at a number of research papers published in academic journals. Such papers are generally reports of empirical research and, while they may be adapted somewhat to meet the requirements of a particular journal, they usually follow the same approximate format.

After the title, it is usual to write an abstract of the project or report. The abstract is typically a single paragraph of about 200 words, which summarises the main features of the study. It should describe briefly the intentions of the study; the methodology used, and the principal findings. From this it is clear that it should be written when the research is completed. Indeed, it may be preferable to write the abstract once the research report is finished, and then to insert it in the text at the beginning.

It is also normal to distinguish the abstract from the remainder of the text by using italics or narrower spacing. It can also be written on an entirely separate sheet of paper and included after the title page of the project.

PRACTICAL ADVICE

When you are writing your abstract, try to think of it as a précis of the entire research report. This is an example of an abstract of a research study in education:

> This is an ethnographic study of a single, large comprehensive school in an urban area. The aim of the study is to describe features of the social and educational lives of pupils, and to explore the interactions of teaching staff, both in the staff room and around the school. The study employs participant observation techniques. The research team consisted of undergraduate students directed by a university lecturer. One of the major findings is that the interaction between staff and pupils during breaks and lunchtimes has a significant effect upon the pupils' attitudes to school.

After the abstract comes the first main section of the report. This can be treated in a number of different ways but the basic function of the section is to outline the purpose of the research and to describe the context in which the research was carried out. It might also say something about the manner in which the research topic was clarified, and the origins of the research idea. You might also want to indicate why you were particulary interested in the issue.

It is sometimes difficult when starting a research report to decide on the tense in which to write. This is resolved to some extent by recognising that the report is written after the event, when the research has been completed. Generally, therefore, the past tense is used, although here and there it may seem more sensible to use the present tense. Personal judgement is needed here. Usually, the correct tense is the one which sounds best.

PRACTICAL ADVICE

When you are writing your introduction, remember that you have the done the research and know all about it; the reader, on the other hand, is completely new to it. Write clearly. Be careful not to miss out important detail, simply because you are familiar with it. Imagine that you are telling a story. Don't rush it, and lead your reader carefully through the events. Here is an example of how the first few lines might be written:

> This is an investigation of the views and attitudes of university students to their Students Union. It was decided to study this aspect of student life because it often seems that students use the Union for certain facilities such as travel tickets, but do not necessarily articulate their views about the staffing and organisation of the union. This no doubt varies from university to university, but given the large number of students, it often seems that only a minority speak up about these issues. The research team decided to adopt a case study approach, selecting three institutions in which to collect data.

A number of subtitles can be used for this section of the report. Some writers simply use 'Introduction', while others might use 'Background and Context'. Another possibility is to use the substantive topic of research in the title, for example 'An Introduction to the nature of Students Unions'. These matters of detail are much less important than the central issue of the writing being clear, and the reader being able to appreciate quickly the purpose of the research.

This introductory section can also include the aims of the research project. These are important because they establish the yardsticks by which the research can be judged. In other words, by the end of the report the reader should be in a position to evaluate the extent to which the aims have been achieved.

The aims can be described in one or two paragraphs which explain the purposes of the research, although it may be difficult to refer to them later in the report. It is frequently easier to set them out as numbered statements, which can be used as easy reference points later.

After the introduction it is normal to provide an overview of the literature in the particular area of the research. A range of different subheadings can be used for this section, for example:

- Review of the literature
- Previous research in the area
- Survey of research in the field
- Research literature

The main feature of the section is that it should show an appreciation of the key contemporary writers and researchers in the field.

> ## *PRACTICAL ADVICE*
>
> In order to locate material to reference, you will need to examine a wide range of sources including indexes of journals, abstracts of dissertations and journals, databases of library stock, interlibrary loan systems, CD-ROMs, and computer network data.
>
> Probably the quickest way for the newcomer to access these sources is first to make a list of the key subject areas of interest. These can be fairly precise, such as 'forest ecology', 'life history research', or 'vitamin synthesis'. The academic librarian in your college or university library should then be able to show you the relevant sources.

After the review of the literature, there is normally the substantive part of the research report. This can be set out in a variety of ways, but it essentially contains an account of how the research was designed, a description of the data collected, and then an analysis of that data. Some writers use the single title 'Methodology' to describe this section, but it is probably better divided up into subsections, each with a more precise heading, for example:

1. Research design
2. Method of data collection
3. Analysis of data
4. Results

Again, there is nothing especially significant about these headings, and others could be substituted, but there is a logic about the sequence of the account. The 'Research design' section deals with the macro issues which were part of the research planning process. In particular, the section will discuss the process by which the aims were transformed into a strategy of action. This section will examine the research population and the definition of samples. It may also discuss the general thought process by which a particular data collection method was selected, and a particular theoretical orientation chosen within which to examine the data.

After this section there is a detailed description of the actual process of data collection. This will include, for example, the procedure for distributing questionnaires, or the arrangements for conducting interviews. Every data collection process necessitates overcoming difficulties or problems of some kind. In the case of questionnaires, the response rate is rarely that which a researcher would ideally hope for; however carefully interviewees are selected, some change their minds at the last minute, or perhaps do not prove to be as co-operative as might have been hoped. This section should discuss the successes of the methodology, and also the shortcomings.

It is worth remembering when writing up a research report, that it does not have to sound as if everything went well. In fact, if it sounds like that, the reader might be inclined to feel rather suspicious! Research is nearly always a process of mixed success. Sometimes things go very well, and sometimes not so well. The failures are just as important as the successes, for the reason that it is often from the failures that we are able to learn.

If respondents do not return many questionnaires, there is usually a reason. It may have been a busy time for those in the sample; the questionnaire may have been too complex and not very user friendly; some of the respondent addresses may have been out of date. We can hypothesise about some of the possible reasons, alter one of the variables and try again. Through this kind of process, we learn a lot about research.

It is far better then to describe the aspects of the research which went as predicted, and also that did not quite go as planned. This kind of open, unbiased account also applies to the ethical aspects of the research. Ethical issues in research are difficult to resolve to the total satisfaction of everyone involved. For example, some researchers feel that they ought to give potential respondents every conceivable opportunity to back out of a research project, and therefore prefer to write to them on the grounds that it is easier for the individual to refuse. Others feel that a personal approach is better, because they can explain the research project in more detail, and hopefully persuade more people to take part. It is almost impossible to resolve this kind of ethical dichotomy. What is important, however, is that these issues are thoroughly and openly discussed, so that the reader of the report can recognise their significance.

In the 'Analysis of data' section, the writer describes the techniques employed to make sense of the primary data, to systematise it, to differentiate the component parts, to synthesise it in a more meaningful way, and to understand the implications of the data. Perhaps the most important requirement of this section is that the writer makes unambiguously clear the analysis procedures used. It is better to describe the method in full, even if it is later proven to have been flawed, than it is to present a sketchy and incomplete account.

PRACTICAL ADVICE

Try to make sure that you describe exactly how you analysed the data. The critical test is whether someone else could take similar data, and, following your description, analyse it in exactly the same way.

The principle here is that all sound research should be capable of being replicated, and the results checked by someone else. This is obviously important in an area such as medical research, but the principle is transferable to all subject areas.

The 'Results' section is the outcome of the data analysis. The results should always be presented in as straightforward a manner as possible. It is probably better to tabulate results or present them as an enumerated list, rather than to embed them in prose. A reader of the research report may need to return to the results on more than one occasion, and it helps considerably if that section is presented in a succinct format. Accompanying the results, there should be a brief statement of any qualifying factors which should be taken into account when reading and applying the results.

A balanced, objective style

To a certain extent, some subject areas have developed their own characteristic ways of reporting research. This is particularly true of what we might term 'methodological schools'. Ethnographic research which aims, amongst other things, to achieve an experiential account of social settings, has experimented with first-person descriptions of events. Similarly, Action Research investigations, which place an emphasis on some of the practical effects of research, have sometimes avoided more conventional ways of presenting research reports.

Generally, however, certain conventions still tend to apply throughout the academic world and the research community. One of the major conventions is to avoid writing as if one's personal feelings and inclinations were instrumental in, say, designing the research strategy. Of course, it is impossible to eliminate subjectivity in the research process, but you can acknowledge all of the diverse influences which are external to the researcher, and explain the significance of these in the way in which the account is written.

PRACTICAL ADVICE

Here are some examples of phrases to avoid when writing a research report. In each numbered example the phrase is italicised in the first sentence, and the second sentence provides a more desirable way of expressing an idea.

1 *I preferred* to use interview techniques because *I felt* that this method would be less stressful for respondents.
This can be rewritten as:
Interview techniques were adopted as these were considered less stressful for respondents.

2 *Personal experience* of surveys *tells me* that response rates rarely exceed 30 per cent.
This can be rewritten as:
There is some evidence that survey response rates rarely exceed 30 per cent.

3 *I believe* that the scientific method cannot really be applied to research with human subjects.
This can be rewritten as:
Some people contend that the scientific method cannot really be applied to research with human subjects.

Writing qualifying statements

In research writing it is important to show that the writer appreciates the limitations of the work which has been carried out. Most research can be described as 'field dependent' or 'context dependent'. This means that although the research findings may appear to have wide applicability, it is difficult for the researcher to know the extent to which the results are a function of the location of the research.

This is easy to appreciate with social science research. If football hooliganism is being investigated at a particular football stadium, there may be many factors peculiar to that stadium which could conceivabley have an effect upon the findings. The design of the stadium, and in particular, the orientation and spacing of the seating might have an effect upon crowd behaviour, but this would be extremely difficult to quantify. Nevertheless, it may be necessary to add riders to the research findings, to demonstrate that the writer has at least an awareness of the possibility.

For example, one might add after the main findings a statement such as:

> It should be noted that these results derive from research at one football stadium only. Although this stadium was selected as being fairly typical for clubs in the division, nevertheless there are some unique features of the stadium which may have affected the research. In particular, it should be noted that the stadium is newly built and has been located some distance from urban housing and outlets for alcohol. This may affect the degree of pre-match consumption of alcohol.

How to write a good conclusion

The conclusion need not add substantially to the results or findings which have already been described in the research report. However, it is normal to draw together the key findings and to provide a brief overview of what has been achieved in the research project. The emphasis should be on brevity.

There is one further aspect of the research which can helpfully be included, and that is suggestions for ways in which the research can be taken further. No research project ever achieves 'the final answers' on a topic, and there is always scope for further investigation. The conclusion is a good place to indicate:

1 Possible strategies for confirming the results of the present investigation;
2 Possible topics for investigation which might shed some light on the periphery of the present issue.

The ability to appreciate such possibilities is evidence that the researcher is thinking on a wider scale than the problems of the immediate research topic.

How will your research report be assessed?

Research reports can be assessed on a number of different levels. Here are some of the questions which the assessor might ask:

1 Does the writer appear to have a clear idea about the purpose of the research, and has this purpose been expressed well in the aims?
2 Is the chosen methodology appropriate for this purpose?
3 Has the methodology been implemented properly?
4 Are the conclusions which have been drawn consistent with the data?
5 Is the report clear and written in a logical sequence?

These criteria generally fall into two groups: those concerned with the *content* of the report; those concerned with the writing and presentation of the report. In different institutions, tutors may place a greater or lesser emphasis on some of these criteria, and this is where it is important for students to take the advice of their lecturers. Nevertheless, the above criteria are likely to be part of the assessment process.

One final consideration is whether the research was designed in such a way as to yield 'interesting' or 'significant' data. This is a difficult criterion to apply because it introduces the subjective element of what should count as 'significant'. In general, it can be argued that 'good' research is 'good' irrespective of the results which happen to be obtained. Here it is the rigour of the methodology which is important, rather then whether the results appear to be particularly exciting.

Summary

- Think carefully about the dissemination of the report.
- Keep the principle of 'informed consent' in mind.
- Consider the issues of confidentiality and anonymity.
- Keep the title brief and relevant.
- The sequence of a research report is important (the actual names of subsections less so)
- Write in the past tense.
- Remember that all sound research should be capable of being replicated.
- Avoid subjective expressions wherever possible.

8
REFERENCING AND BIBLIOGRAPHIES

In academic writing there is a long-established tradition of referring to the writing or research of other academics. This practice shows that the writer is aware of other scholarship in the field and acknowledges that, in some cases, someone else had the idea before. It also enables the reader to check what the writer is saying against the ideas of others.

This latter function is important as it provides reassurance for the reader that what is being said is not in isolation from other contemporary thought. This is not to say, however, that everything must be in agreement with what has gone before, and that there cannot be new ideas. Even in the case of the avant-garde or radically new ideas, it should still be possible to relate these to previous developments and to show how the new has built upon the old.

Reference to other works can also provide illustrative matter which perhaps enlivens or enhances what is being written. A sharp, witty quotation from a famous person may serve this function. It may not add significantly to the essential argument, but it can make the writing more humorous or demonstrate that the idea being discussed has wide currency. Other kinds of references can literally illustrate what is being written. If a particular investigation is being described in an essay or report, then it may be possible to refer to other similar investigations in the past.

A suitable reference may also be used to substantiate an argument which is being advanced by the writer. Suppose that it is being suggested in an essay that social cohesion has been gradually declining in England since the Second World War, then perhaps the argument can be strengthened by reference to several noted historians who have adopted the same view. Clearly, this kind of support for arguments does not make the argument absolutely true, it may merely add some weight to it. The crucial issue is the kind of evidence upon which the noted historians have constructed their arguments.

Referencing, then, does not 'prove' arguments, but it may 'support' and 'enhance' them. As such, it is an important feature of academic writing, and should be used wherever appropriate.

There are several different ways in which we can refer to other writers and their works. These divide into the following main categories:

- using a direct, verbatim quotation and integrating it into the text of the essay or report
- referring the reader to a key writer and his or her work.
- providing a reading list or bibliography of relevant works

The particular type of reference used depends upon the type of work. A highly scholarly work may employ many short quotations to demonstrate the links with other research. More general works such as essays or projects may refer to writers and also employ a reading list. The subject matter may also affect the style of referencing. A highly specialised subject may require many precise references, while for a more general subject a reading list may be appropriate.

In the case of college and university assignments, considerable attention is given to referencing and bibliographies during assessment. The reason for this is that it is used by the tutor as an indicator of familiarity with the literature and breadth of reading. It is worthwhile giving considerable attention to referencing, and making sure that the works referred to are as relevant and contemporary as possible.

Selecting a suitable extract

Suitable extracts are not always easy to find, and considerable work may be involved. A good extract should conform to a number of basic requirements. The first of these is that it should be *understandable* when it is removed from its original context. In a piece of prose, most sentences relate to both the preceding and the following sentences. To remove a sentence from its context, can all too often remove much of its sense. A good quotation retains this sense, when inserted into the essay, project or research report.

Sometimes, in order to select an appropriate quotation, it is necessary to subdivide a sentence and to use only a part of it. For example,

> Professor Jones suggests that: 'The profiles of such valleys are most easily explained by glaciation, rather than other geophysical causes . . .'

The dots indicate that an incomplete sentence has been used. It is important to acknowledge this because it is so easy to take a quotation and to use it out of context, thereby changing its meaning. This is obviously unfair to the original writer. A quotation should be used as far as possible so that the original meaning (as far as this can reasonably be ascertained) is retained. There is a particular danger of transforming the meaning when only part of a sentence is used, and therefore a significant aspect of the sense is omitted. The dots indicate this to the reader, and openly and honestly demonstrate what has been done. Should there be any doubt about the full meaning, then the reader is able to check this by using the reference in the bibliography.

The suitable quotation should also be *representative* of the writer in question. There is an important ethical issue here. It is not particularly difficult to take from a book an extract which, although accurate, does not really represent the general viewpoint or perspective of the writer. Although this may not involve a technical infringement of what one can legitimately do, it is certainly against the spirit of using quotations.

This could also be done through a genuine mistake, caused by not reading the book thoroughly, or not understanding the theoretical position of the writer. It is clearly best for several reasons, to try to ensure that the quotation used is typical of the work or stance of a particular writer.

The other important criteria for quotations are *length* and *quantity*. When considering the length of a quotation to use, and also the number to select, it is important to remember the basic principle that quotations should be secondary to the main text. They are there to provide examples for the main text; to illustrate and amplify the main text; to provide material for the writer to analyse in the main text. They are there to *serve* the main text, rather than the other way round.

It is extremely difficult to provide a rigid rule about length and quantity, not least because different sections of an assignment have different requirements. The literature survey of a research report may need a lot of short quotations in order to provide illustrative material. An English literature essay may require one or two long quotations in order to provide material for textual analysis. The main criterion should be that the quotations do not detract too much from the main text.

> *PRACTICAL ADVICE*
>
> Clearly the criteria for length can only be general guidance, but I would suggest that you try to keep quotations to between forty to eighty words in length; and if necessary use about one or two to the page. Having said that, some pages may not have any quotations, and others may have three or four.

Writing the introduction

A quotation should not suddenly appear in a piece of text without an introduction of some kind. Otherwise, it breaks the flow of the prose, and disrupts the argument being developed by the writer. The reader is usually interested in two things about a quotation – the *content* and the *person who has written it*. The latter is usually a significant feature in the choice of the extract, and provides a means of introducing the quotation. The reader is usually interested in anything about the writer of the quotation. The following are some examples of the way in which introductions might be written:

> Professor Mary Jones, a leading cognitive psychologist, has suggested the following framework for concept formation:
>
> Dr David Jones, of the Northern University, has consistently argued for a wider dissemination of medical research findings in this field:
>
> Dr Susan Jones, who was the first sociologist to use this term, wrote in this seminal work:

It is helpful to try to vary the manner in which quotations are introduced, so that the text does not become too predictable.

Page layout

There are three types of referencing in common use in academic writing, and these are:

1 The reference to an author and the date of the relevant publication. There is no quotation in the text, but the full details of the publication are included in the bibliography;
2 The use of a short quotation. When this is part of a sentence (say one or two lines), it is usually incorporated in the main text, without indenting. The name of the author and the date of publication are added at a convenient point in the main text, as in 1 above;
3 The use of a long quotation of several sentences. This is usually indented, or offset from the main text in some way. Some writers use italics or closer spacing to distinguish the quotation from the main text. Again, the name of the author and the date of publication are added.

If we now look at examples of each type, it should become clear that there is a uniformity underlying the general system. The simplest way of referencing is to refer to the author alone, without a quotation. An example is:

> It is argued that the teaching of science by using heuristic or 'discovery' methods has many advantages and, in particular, encourages pupils to think systematically about the world in which they find themselves. The opportunity to understand in practice, the interplay between variables is regarded by some writers as being very significant (Smith, 1990 and Jones, 1991).

This reference tells us that the works by Smith and Jones will discuss the issue mentioned in the final sentence. The actual works can be identified from the bibliography. Sometimes, a page number is added after the year of publication in the text. The page number can also be added after the full details in the bibliography. The omission of a page number in the example above suggests that the issue of understanding scientific variables is discussed generally throughout the works mentioned. The addition of a page number would suggest that the discussion of the issue is restricted to certain parts of the works only.

This kind of referencing is quick and easy to use, and tends to be employed particularly where an overview of a large area of study is required. It is then possible to refer to a large number of authors within a relatively small space.

The next type of reference is where a short quotation is employed. If a short extract was separated from the main text, it would tend to break up the prose too much, and such quotations are usually incorporated in the normal text. An example is as follows:

> The art of calligraphy is more than mere technique, and more than mere artistry with brush or pen. Calligraphy says something about the words which are its subject. The word is a symbol and 'its form is an integral component of the concept for which it stands' (Thomson, 1994, p.33).

Quotations such as this can be as short as a single word, where for example, it is necessary to quote a particular term or concept which has been used elsewhere. Where a quotation cannot be incorporated easily into a single sentence of the main text, then it is probably better to treat it completely separately.

Longer quotations are normally set outin the as following way.

> It is possible to view an educational system in purely functionalist terms. Within this perspective, education can be seen as training, socialising and even conditioning a future workforce to ensure the economic stability of society. Baker (1993, p.46) considers that this is a limited vision:
>
> > *Education is more than preparation for economic productivity. It is about understanding the world in which we live, and learning to interact with that world in an ethical manner. It is about understanding different forms of thought and different visions of the potential of humanity.*
>
> This wider view of education does not deny the importance of preparation for the world of work, but does not accord it the importance attached to it by the functionalist.

The main feature of this form of layout is that the quotation is separated from the main text, and identified by using a different print style or by different line spacing. As long as these main functions are achieved, then there is scope for a number of variations in presentation. These can include:

- The quotation is usually separated from the main text by wider line spacing at the beginning and end;
- The quotation can also be indented. This is can be done at the left-hand margin only, or at both left-hand and the right-hand margins.
- The quotation can be printed in a smaller font size;
- The quotation can be printed in a different font style to the main text. This is usually italic;
- The quotation can have different line spacing from the main text.

The main purpose of this type of layout is to avoid any ambiguity about the origin of the quotation, and to emphasise that it has been written by someone else than the main writer.

Using the Harvard System

The system of referencing described above constitutes the essentials of the Harvard System. This referencing procedure is simple and straightforward, and is the most common system used in contemporary books and journals. The essential idea is to give the author's surname, year of publication (and sometimes page number) in the text, and then to list the full bibliographic details of the work at the end of the assignment.

In slightly older books or journals, a numbering system can be found. In this system, each quotation is allocated a number in sequence throughout the chapter or book. There is then a numerical list of full bibliographic details at the end of the chapter. The great difficulty with such a system is that it is easy to number quotations in an incorrect sequence which does not relate to the bibliographic list at the end of the assignment. This is particularly so when it is necessary to insert an extra quotation after the main piece of work has been completed. It is probably wiser to avoid this system of referencing in assignments.

Within the Harvard System several minor refinements are necessary to deal with more unusual circumstances. It may be necessary in an essay or report to refer to two different works by the same author which have been published in the same year. This may give rise to some confusion and is avoided by using lower case 'a' and 'b' as in the following example:

> Johnson (1995a) provides a general account of Arctic ecosystems, while in a subsequent publication (1995b) she describes the result of a long-term study of the musk ox in the northern Canadian tundra.

The lower case 'a' and 'b' are then repeated in the bibliography in order to distinguish the two books or research studies.

Sometimes a book has joint authors, and this is easily indicated by writing something such as (Jones and Johnson, 1995). In the less usual case of a book having three authors, then it can be referenced as (Jones and others, 1995) or, if there is a preference for Latin, (Jones *et al*, 1995). Where it is necessary to refer to a chapter in an edited book or to an article in a journal, then the author of the chapter or article is referenced in the text.

We have now examined the Harvard System from the point of view of the textual references, so we need now to think about the list of works at the end of the essay or assignment. This list of works can be entitled 'Bibliography' or 'References'.

Up to a point, these two terms seem to be used interchangeably, but perhaps they can be distinguished on the following grounds. A list entitled 'References' would normally include only those works which are actually referred to in the main text. If a list is entitled 'Bibliography' then the assumption is that it contains works which are relevant to the subject matter of the assignment, but which are not necessarily referred to in the text. Although the point does not seem to be particularly critical, one solution is to include at the end of an assignment two lists, one of works referred to, and the other of supplementary reading material.

However, whichever term is used, there are certainly conventions about the way in which works are listed. The general rule is that they are listed by alphabetical order of author surname. In addition, different categories of works, such as for example, books or journal articles, are described in different ways. The three principal categories, are described on pages 123 and 124.

1 Authored books

These are described in the list of references as shown in the following example:

Gardener, H (1990) *The Ecology of Wet Meadowlands*, Aberdeen, Southern University Press

It is normal to print the book title in italics. If the assignment is handwritten, then the convention is to underline the title. When naming the author, the full first name or simply the initial, may be used. The order for the reference is as follows:

- surname of author
- initial (or first name)
- year of publication
- title of book
- place of publication (with state/province if overseas)
- publisher

2 Chapter in an edited book

Most academic edited books consist of chapters each written by a different author, but linked together by a common theme. The editor or editors will normally write an introductory chapter which explains the theme of the book. A single chapter is referenced as follows:

Shield, J (1987) 'The Roman campaigns in the Pennine hills', in P Magnus (ed.) *The Roman Legions in Britain*, Southampton, Australia Press

The main point to note is that the chapter author and chapter title are given before the name of the editor and book title. The date of publication will normally be the same for all the chapters in the book (i.e. the same as the book publication date). The other significant point is that it is the book title which is italicised, and not the chapter title. The order then, is as follows:

- surname of chapter author
- initial (or first name)
- year of publication
- title of chapter (in normal font)
- initial (or first name) of book editor
- Surname of book editor
- (ed.)

- Title of book (in italics)
- Place of publication
- Publisher

A minor point to note is that normally the initial precedes the surname of the book editor.

3 Article in a journal

These are referenced as in the following example:

> Coker, S (1975) 'A History of the Atlantic Steamer', *Journal of Steam Ships and Liners*, 6, pp.217–230

The title of the journal, rather than the article title, is printed in italics. The number after the journal title is the volume number. The page numbers refer to the beginning and end of the article. The sequence of the entry is, therefore, as follows:

- surname of article author
- initial (or first name)
- year of publication
- title of article
- title of journal (in italics)
- volume number of journal
- page numbers of the article

It is also perhaps worth noting briefly that a research dissertation can be referenced as follows: Shelf, J (1971) The Monastic Library. Unpublished PhD dissertation. University of Scotland.

Other styles of referencing

The three styles above are the main types of references which are most commonly needed by students writing assignments. There are however, many variations on these themes; for example, where the author is not recorded as a person, but as, say, a government department. It is probably not worth trying to document all of these permuatations. Trying to establish definite rules for every conceivable variation and format of publication is difficult, and in any case, individual academics do employ slightly different approaches to presenting bibliographies. The three basic forms illustrated above should provide a format for dealing with most types of published work.

PRACTICAL ADVICE

It is a good idea to use the Harvard system if you can, because it is straightforward and does include all of the necessary information about a publication. However, the two basic principles of referencing are worth remembering:

1 Be consistent, within the same piece of work;
2 Include all of the relevant information.

It can sometimes seem as if all the emphasis on the minutiae of referencing, is unnecessary. However, the basic purpose is to ensure that all the relevant information is included and that the reader of the assignment or essay can trace the actual quotation if so desired. In most cases no-one will wish to do this, but from time to time someone may be interested in a particular book or article and will seek out the original. It is important that you give them sufficient information to enable them to do this whenever they wish.

The other principle is, of course, that in all academic writing it is important to declare accurately the sources of our quotations. It is part of the open and objective spirit of rational enquiry.

Avoiding plagiarism

The rule about using the writing of someone else, can be kept fairly simple: If you wish to use what someone else has written in your own assignment, then use the referencing system described above.

The only possible area of ambiguity is in a situation where a common word or term is given a specialised meaning and significance by a particular writer. An example might be the use of the word 'power' in sociology. Clearly this word can be used in an everyday sense in ordinary language, but within sociology it acquires different connotations depending upon its use by individual sociologists. If it is used in an assignment within the context of one of these specialist uses, then arguably it should be enclosed within quotation marks. This is perhaps a fine point and much depends upon the extent to which the use may be regarded as specialist. There is room for a certain amount of interpretation here.

Besides using a referencing system such as the Harvard System, the other main strategy for minimising the risk of plagiarism is to paraphrase material. The act of paraphrasing is to take a piece of original writing and to rewrite it in your own words and from your own angle. Paraphrasing is indeed an art. It demands a sound understanding of the original passage, and the capacity to express the same ideas in a different way.

The essence of paraphrasing is to take the holistic view of a passage, and to represent the ideas and concepts in different language. The crucial issue is whether paraphrased material should be referenced in any way. The answer is that it probably depends upon the nature of the original material.

PRACTICAL ADVICE

If you feel that the material you are paraphrasing expresses ideas which have been uniquely articulated by an individual writer, then it is probably better to indicate the origin of the ideas, even if you have expressed them in your own words. Your writing would then take on a form such as the following:

> The idea that research on management should focus particularly on the personal experiences of those managed, has been notably advocated by Peterson (1967). She suggested that interview data was especially crucial in this respect.

Notice here that there are no quotation marks, because all the material is paraphrased. However, the author reference is included, because the student has decided that this approach to management research is particularly associated with this writer.

If general material is paraphrased, there is probably less obligation to indicate the sources. This is a common situation with students writing essays. A text book is consulted in order to understand a topic, and then the material is paraphrased for the essay. This is perfectly acceptable, as long as the material is of a general nature. Even then, however, it may still be desirable to mention some sources, as this adds to the academic credibility of what is written.

When paraphrasing it is clearly unnecessary to paraphrase technical terms in a particular subject area. If this were done, then it would almost certainly destroy the meaning of the rewritten passage.

In general, it is probably advisable to provide references for paraphrased passages and to restrict the quantity of paraphrasing. After all, an assignment should be largely a student's own, unique work.

— Creating an index of references —

Assembling a list of references for an assignment can become quite an onerous task if carried out separately for each assignment. It is an activity which lends itself best to a progressive strategy throughout a course. It has been suggested elsewhere that a directory of quotations can be assembled, and used as necessary. This kind of approach can also be used for assembling annotated bibliographies.

Within a defined subject area, it is useful to have a list of books and journal articles which have been consulted, and which may be used again for future assignments. The difficulty with a simple list is that it is easy to forget the key features of each book. An annotated bibliography includes a few brief notes on the characteristics of each publication which are particularly noteworthy. This is a great help in compiling future bibliographies for assignments.

PRACTICAL ADVICE

When you start your course, try to get into the habit of making brief notes on every book or article which you consult. You will probably not read all of each book, but will be able to note down the things which have interested you. It is also a good idea to note the decimal reference number of the book in the library. This will help you to locate the publication quickly in future.

The ideal way to record your bibliography is on a single computer disk. Most modern software has the capacity to order entries in alphabetical order, and in this way you can build up a learning resource which will be of inestimable use.

Do remember, however, to check the alphabetical order as

some programs do not, for example, allow for the fact that 'Mc' should treated the same as 'Mac'

The following would be a typical kind of entry in your annotated bibliography:

Paulinson, T (1988) *The contribution of the Impressionists to modern art,* Manchester, Eastern University Press

Notes: a very readable book; excellent colour illustrations. The chapter on Monet includes details of his early life. Sets the Impressionists in the context of other Schools. Worth looking at again.

Constructing a bibliography

When constructing a bibliography or list of references for an essay or report, it is not always possible to locate books and articles which are exactly connected with the topic. It is sometimes necessary to include publications which are less centrally connected with the research issue. To take an example here, we might consider a research topic such as the distribution of women in management positions within a group of organisations. It will almost certainly be possible to locate literature on 'women in management', but perhaps there will not be as many publications as one might hope for. Other publications could be used, for example on the general subject of organisational management, on gender, and on appraisal and promotion procedures.

Sometimes it is appropriate to subdivide a bibliography into such separate sections. The works in each subsection are listed in alphabetical order. This format can help the reader to appreciate the works listed in a more systematic way. For similar reasons, some writers subdivide a bibliography into books, journal articles and, say, internal or unpublished source material. There is a certain amount of scope here for a sensible use of categories.

Summary

- You can refer to other writers by direct quotation, noting the name of the writer, or by providing a supplementary reading list.
- Try not to let quotations disrupt the flow of your writing.
- Introduce quotations smoothly.
- Use a standard system of referencing.
- Be consistent.
- Provide all relevant referencing information.
- Always provide a reference for a direct quotation.
- Consider building up your own annotated bibliography.

9
LINKING THEORY AND PRACTICAL EXAMPLES

'Theory' and 'theoretical arguments' generally have quite a poor image. There is a tendency to associate theory with abstract thought far removed from the 'real' world. Theory is often assumed to be the province of academics and professors who sit in 'ivory towers', and are unconcerned about practical issues. Theories are perhaps seen as being 'clever' but generally of little use in solving everyday problems. They are probably seen by many people as a luxury.

It is perhaps true to say that there is a dichotomy in the minds of many people, between 'theory' and 'practice'. The two are seen as different activities, which have little interrelationship. This is actually far from the truth, and it is rather a pity that there is this image of theory. In fact, theory is based on practice and upon practical observations.

How theory is created

We can illustrate this by thinking about one of the best-known theories, the Theory of Gravity. Every pupil comes across this at school, and indeed, we are so familiar with the idea of gravity that perhaps we take it for granted. The Theory of Gravity is wonderful in its simplicity. It states that there is a force of attraction between two bodies which depends upon both the masses of the bodies concerned and the distance between them. The greater the masses, the greater the force. The greater the distance between the bodies, the less the force. The useful aspect of this theory is that is seems to operate not just on Earth, but elsewhere in the universe as well. In other words it is generally applicable.

This theory was not developed by scientists sitting in an ivory tower, totally removed from the world. Isaac Newton made careful observations of the world around him, and then thought systematically about how these observations might be explained by a single, coherent principle. Without the observation that objects 'fall' to earth, or that planetary bodies are apparently 'held' in orbit by a force, there would almost certainly have been no theory of gravity. The theory is based upon practical experience, or, as it is often termed in science, empirical observation.

Having taken a specific example of a theory with which most people are familiar, it should be possible to clarify some of the key features. A theory:

- consists of a set of statements or propositions which are normally capable of being tested against experience
- should normally be capable of predicting future events (within the area of the theory)
- should be capable of (to some extent) providing an explanation for empirical observations
- should ideally be simple and straightforward, but should be capable of being applied in a variety of different contexts

The Theory of Gravity appears to fulfil each of these criteria to a greater or lesser extent. The theory can be tested against experience, because we can observe what happens when objects are dropped, or when bodies in outer space move nearer to each other. Linked to this is the notion of prediction. The theory enables us to predict future events, such as the results of knocking a china cup off the edge of a table which is standing on a hard floor. So reliable does this theory appear to be, that we take it into account at all times, when conducting our daily lives. We do not step out of a window on the twentieth floor, in order to appreciate the view a little better.

The Theory of Gravity as stated above goes some way towards meeting the third characteristic of a theory, that of providing explanation. Much depends, however, on our understanding of the word 'explanation'. We may observe a change in orbit of a planetary body, and 'explain' this by means of the Theory of Gravity. To what extent the theory 'explains' the nature of gravity is a different question. Finally, the theory is straightforward and easy to understand, and can certainly be applied in a variety of different situations.

Another crucial aspect of a theory is that, no matter how effective it has been in terms of explaining and predicting events, it is important to acknowledge that it may not be effective in the future. It may not seem probable, but the cup which overbalances on the table, one day may not fall to the ground, but may remain suspended in the air! If this did happen then the Theory of Gravity would require revising to take into account this remarkable observation. The important principle here is that a theory is only as good as the last observation which supports it. There is always the possibility of a new observation which cannot be explained by the theory.

This idea reinforces the temporary and provisional nature of theories. There is a tendency to think of theories enshrined in text books, as immutable statements about the nature of the universe. On this model, the main purpose of research is to find data which supports existing theory. It is more logical, however, to think of research as seeking examples of events which invalidate theories. This model emphasises the idea that we are not certain about the nature of the world, and that theories are our attempts at trying to create a sense of order.

Science, whether natural science or social science, is an attempt to create general statements about the world, which are useful for prediction and explanation. Moreover, such statements are seen as essentially provisional, and subject to continual review and amendment. This view of scientific method is far reaching and has extensive implications for the way in which theory is integrated into assignments, and the way in which language is employed in essays and reports. Within this perspective it is clearly important that theories are not treated as if they represent an absolute truth, or a yardstick against which everything can be measured. Rather, they should be regarded as useful integrative statements, which can help in making sense of data, and in generating testable propositions for further research.

Selecting appropriate theory

Having examined something of the nature of theory, it is worth considering why it can be helpful to employ theory in writing essays and reports. We can distinguish between two related concepts, 'theory' and 'perspective'.

A perspective is a particular way of viewing the world and of interpreting data. For example, in social science one quite frequently comes across the idea of a 'conflict' perspective, and a 'consensus' perspective. The conflict perspective assumes that within society there are individuals, groups, and organisations who are all competing with each other for power, wealth or influence. Some of those who subscribe to this perspective may feel that such conflict is to some extent functional for society, in that it binds people together in a network of competition. The consensus perspective on the other hand, assumes that, to a large extent, people and organisations work towards harmonious relations, even if these are not always achieved. Again, many adherents would no doubt feel that consensus is largely functional for society, and supports social cohesion.

Individuals who look at society from each of these two viewpoints may emphasise different aspects of the world around them. The consensus perspective will stress examples of harmony and concord, while the conflict perspective will emphasise instances of discord, even when basically the same situation is being examined. At the risk of being accused of oversimplification, we might say that we see in situations what we want to see.

The perspective then, is a broad viewpoint on the world, and within a perspective there exists a large number of theories. These theories, as has been said above, consist of relationships between variables and concepts, such that the theory is generally able to provide explanations and predictions about the world. We do not necessarily have to rely upon scientists or academics to develop theories for us. We can generate our own theory from observations of the world around us – indeed we often do. Anyone who drives to work for instance will probably find him or herself producing theories about traffic flow. Such a theory might be something like this:

> Traffic flow rate depends on the time of day and the time of the week, and is particularly related to people's work patterns. Monday morning and Friday evening are especially busy because people are either beginning or concluding longer work journeys.

Car drivers probably construct many other theories to incorporate such features as roadworks, weather conditions, and presence of heavy vehicles. Just like the theory of gravity, such theories have an explanatory function and a predictive function. Moreover, drivers use their own theories to try to make their journeys faster and less stressful. If the theory proves unable to predict road conditions, then it is quickly changed by the driver. The adapted theory is then tested on another day to see whether it helps to create a more congenial journey.

Such theories help drivers to make sense of the apparently random nature of road traffic and to start to understand some of the patterns which emerge. Much is the same with theories in academic writing. The theory, and the perspective within which it is located, both help in making sense of data, in systematising it, and in presenting it coherently to the world. The choice of theory and perspective is important. It depends upon the kind of analysis which we hope to achieve in our essay or report, and also upon the subjective approach which we bring to our work.

As an example, consider an essay on art appreciation, and particularly the nature of response to modern, abstract art. In fact, it might be possible to write such an essay from a strictly scientific perspective, or from what we might term an 'aesthetic' perspective. The scientific perspective might focus particularly upon the texture of a painting; the way light is reflected differentially from surfaces of different texture; the way types of paint contribute to texture; the way an artist may have employed different types of material to produce a particular texture. The scientific perspective may also focus upon the practical applications of abstract designs, and the possibilities of employing them in, say, architecture or other technological contexts. In other words, the abstract painting is examined from a particular point of view, taking into account such aspects as textural and structural features.

On the other hand, a painting could equally well be explored from an aesthetic perspective, taking into account the effect which the painting has on the observer: perhaps the sense of peace or stillness which it creates; the interrelationship between the colours which have been selected; and the suggestions of form in the design of the painting. The painting remains the same painting, but it is examined in a totally different way.

An essay about abstract art written from a scientific perspective would be different from an essay written within an aesthetic frame of reference. The two essays would employ different concepts and would focus upon different understandings of paintings.

It would also be possible within one of these perspectives to write from the point of view of a particular theory. For example, within the aesthetic perspective we might examine a theory of 'abstract art as meditation'. Such a theory might develop the idea that looking at art can create a particularly peaceful frame of mind, and that in this sense art is extremely functional on a psychological level. An essay written within such a theory might also point to evidence such as religious symbols used as objects of contemplation.

The theory then becomes a framework within which one can place examples, and within which arguments can be developed. It can be an integrating mechanism in an essay, enable a sense of cohesion to be given to what might otherwise be fairly disparate ideas.

Interrelating theory with practical examples

When writing an assignment it is not always easy to think of practical examples with which to support a theoretical argument. One of the best ways is to turn to books or articles which have been written within the framework of a particular theory. There can, however, be a problem in identifying the theoretical basis from which a book is written. It may be necessary to read most of a book before getting clues as to the theoretical orientation of the author.

It can be argued that it behoves authors who are writing from a particular viewpoint to explain this in the introduction to the book. This is really in the spirit of openness of academic writing. If a particular theoretical viewpoint has significantly affected the way in which subject matter is presented, then it can be argued that this should be specifically indicated. The vast majority of academic writers do this as a matter of course, and this provides a useful strategy for students who are trying to assemble examples to illustrate a particular theoretical viewpoint.

> *PRACTICAL ADVICE*
>
> When you are writing an essay or assignment around a particular theory, it helps to provide examples from writers who have employed that theoretical orientation.
>
> Examine books or articles for clues as to the theory used. Sometimes the evidence is in the title of the work, and sometimes in the introduction. A rapid survey of publications in this way saves time when selecting examples to quote.

Avoiding jargon

The purpose of good academic writing is really the same as that of any other form of writing, and that purpose is to communicate ideas. It can sometimes seem as if terminology gets in the way of this purpose, and makes academic writing obscure and appear to exist only for the initiated.

The difficulty with specialist vocabulary is that it is specialist, and presumably one requires an element of induction into the language. However, it is important to ensure that specialist vocabulary is used solely to convey precise ideas, and not to attempt to make the language sound more 'academic' or 'clever' or to show off or patronise your readers.

When discussing theory and theories it can be easy to slip into using long and apparently complex words, which on closer examination may not have a precise meaning in a particular context. The use of such words can be self-defeating, because it can so easily impair communication. A brief selection of words may serve as an illustration:

estrangement
depersonalisation
disorientation
objectification
self-consciousness
self-determination
primitivism

If such words are used, not as technical terms, but in ordinary writing, the meaning may be obscured. The reason can be because words such as these are employed to summarise complex ideas which really require much more explanation. Consider the following sentence which uses several of the above words:

> The estrangement of the individual from the norms of society may result in a diminished self-consciousness, and an inability to view one's situation with any sense of objectification.

Now on one level, this sentence is grammatical and appears to have meaning. It certainly sounds rather grand and profound. However, is it possible to be really sure of the ideas which the writer is trying to convey? This sentence would probably be much more effective if the ideas it contained were conveyed in a number of simpler sentences which gave the reader the opportunity to understand properly what was being said.

PRACTICAL ADVICE

Don't try to make your writing sound extra 'academic' just for the sake of it. Have a clear idea in your mind of what you want to say, and then express it in the clearest possible language. Use technical or specialist vocabulary only when this is necessary in order to express a specific concept.

— Can you give your own opinions? —

In the context of academic writing, this can be a difficult issue to resolve. The response to the question might well be, 'It depends on what you mean by opinions'.

It is normally difficult to isolate our feelings and emotions about issues, to set them on one side, and to write an essay or assignment in an absolutely clinical way, balancing arguments and issues with total objectivity. Suppose one is writing an essay about a government's financial policy towards helping certain disadvantaged groups. If one has a strong sense of empathy for some of these groups, and it is evident that more money would help the situation, then it may be difficult to hide one's feelings when writing the assignment. Even if one does not make overt statements criticising national policy, it may well be that one's viewpoint can hardly be hidden. It may emerge in the kind of evidence which is selected, and in the manner in which it is presented. The writing may be such that one could not be accused of bias or distortion, but nevertheless, the viewpoint may still emerge.

In some forms of writing, including serious journalism, it is common (and indeed necessary) at times, to express one's own viewpoint. In academic writing, however, there is a fine line between allowing a sense of conviction on an issue to emerge in the writing, and producing a piece of work which is clearly biased.

The best solution is probably to try to be absolutely open about a situation where a personal viewpoint is being expressed. It might be, for example, that an essay is contrasting two entirely different theoretical approaches to a topic, yet the writer actually feels that one approach is much more relevant that the other. In this case it is probably better to contrast the theories in as objective a manner as possible, and then to express one's own feelings when this process has been completed. It should be clear to the reader, that the analysis is moving from an objective contrasting of theories, to a subjective statement on behalf of the writer. If this clear distinction is made, then there can be little objection.

Writing about anecdotes

There is often a temptation when discussing theories, to try to support a theoretical position by resource to anecdotes. We might write sentences such as:

> My own observations of this tend to support the theory.
>
> When I conducted the same experiment, it soon became clear that the results were similar.

> Field data collected during my own research tends to support this idea.
>
> When I was on my work placement, I collected very similar data.

There are two difficulties with this kind of anecdotal writing. First, as we have discussed above under the nature of theory, one extra piece of evidence does not 'prove' a theory. We must be cautious about thinking that a single piece of anecdotal evidence can do anything else than simply support and supplement existing corroborative data. Second, the application of *personal* data in relation to a theory, rather than the use of data deriving from others, can be seen as less than objective.

— Writing restrained conclusions —

Theories are helpful human constructions for making the world more understandable and meaningful. They are however, *human* constructions. The 'Theory of Gravity' does not exist somewhere out there in the world – it exists in the minds of human beings. It helps us to understand things better. It helps us to make sense of our surroundings and the things which we observe. Theories can be changed whenever they do not seem to fit their purpose. Theories are only as good as the last observation which supports them.

Therefore, we should not have too much misplaced respect for theories. Many theories may be associated with great thinkers, either from the past or present, but we should remember that all theories share the notion that they are provisional. When we are writing conclusions we should bear in mind this provisional nature of knowledge. Data can *support* or *lend credence* to theory; data can *fail to support* theory; but data can never *prove* theory.

Summary

- Theories are 'grounded' in empirical observations.
- Theories have both a predictive and explanatory function.
- Generating theories is a common feature of the thought process.
- There is no virtue in trying to make writing seem complex, just for effect.
- Use personal opinion and anecdote extremely carefully.

10
CHECKING AND EDITING

Teachers and lecturers are generally in the business of education because they enjoy teaching and working with students. Most tutors like being asked for help, and up to a certain point will gladly give of their time outside classes to provide informal advice. However, these days they have much more to do than teaching and assessing work, and there are many professional calls on their time. However much they might like to provide unlimited tutorial time, it is just unrealistic. Students will generally get the most effective and efficient advice from tutors if they go with a specific task or problem, rather than seek open-ended discussion time.

Help from your tutor

Take a small section of an assignment for a tutor to read and comment on. The section need be no more than one or two pages. It often happens in the early stages of an assignment that students have uncertainties about either subject matter or approach to writing. The best approach is probably to write a rough draft of the difficult section and give it to the tutor to read. The tutor may prefer to take it away for checking, because the task can be easily fitted in among other responsibilities. A time can be arranged for feedback from tutor to student. The feedback can be quick, and a system such as this is most time effective for both parties concerned. When tutors are not commenting on a complete assignment, they may feel able to write suggestions on the short draft. They may consider that this falls within the remit of ongoing tutorial advice, and does not unnecessarily favour one student more than another.

One advantage of this system is that the tutor can identify either knowledge or stylistic errors when they first emerge in an assignment, and the student can avoid these mistakes later on in the work.

PRACTICAL ADVICE

Try to make the most cost-effective use of both your own time and that of your tutor. Remember that your tutor may have no time on the allocated timetable for tutorials outside normal classes. When asking for help:

- ask for an appointment time, and give some indication of the extent of the enquiry
- be punctual
- be brief and stick to the point
- if you think you might need further advice, ask if that will be possible
- if you asked for fifteen minutes of time, leave when the time is up
- if you use good time management skills with tutors, they will be much more willing to see you again

What your tutor can and cannot do

One of the important ethical aspects of a tutor's job is to try to be even-handed in giving advice, and to avoid providing significantly more help for one student than another. The key word here is 'significantly'. Let us assume for the sake of argument, that a unit of work has been completed, and students are now working on their assignment, with the opportunity for further limited contact with the tutor.

Some students may not ask for any further assistance from their tutor, and may simply complete the assignment and hand it in. On the other hand, some may ask for varying degrees of help. The tutor's job is to provide appropriate assistance, but not to the extent that one individual is helped significantly in comparison with another. Tutors will probably try to achieve this difficult balancing act by keeping advice as general as possible.

Tutors should not be asked for a prediction of the grade for a particular assignment, before the formal submission process. Tutors will not wish to give any kind of informal judgement on grades. Often, more than one tutor is involved in assessment, and it would be inappropriate to give an informal opinion. External examiners may also be involved. However anxious students are about a particular assignment, they should submit the assignment in the standard way and await the outcome. There should not, however, be an undue wait for the result. Most institutions have a timescale within which assessment will take place, and students are entitled to expect that normally tutors will adhere to this.

Presentation and layout

One of the difficulties with academic writing is the maintenance of consistency. This is not difficult with a short piece of work, but with a longer assignment it is hard to achieve. Consistency is also easier to maintain when a piece of work is written in only one or two sessions. When an assignment is written in a lot of different sections over a period of time, it is difficult to maintain consistency in layout, writing style, and approach. One of the purposes of final editing is to remove some of these variations where they have an adverse effect upon the cohesion of the writing.

The process of editing can be quite difficult and tedious. It is not easy to read a long assignment, and search out errors of content and argument, while simultaneously looking for spelling and syntax errors, and ways of improving layout. One strategy is to try to divide up the editing process into sections. The assignment can be read in two stages. The first reading can be devoted to looking for errors of content, such as omissions of significant work and errors in logic; the second reading can be devoted to layout, spelling and grammar. The tasks can be subdivided in other ways, but the principle of carrying out one type of editing at a time is a helpful idea.

PRACTICAL ADVICE

The first thing to do when editing an assignment is to have another look through the official style notes or guidelines for the assignment. Ask yourself:

- Have I answered the question or title?
- Have I written the required amount?
- Have I put all the necessary information on the cover sheet?
- Have I made the margins the correct width?
- Have I written a 'Contents' page?
- Have I numbered all the pages?

A final look through lecture notes can be helpful at the start of the editing stage. There may be a key writer who has not been covered in the assignment; or a piece of advice from the tutor may have been overlooked. The great advantage of word processors is that such last-minute changes or additions can be made without adversely affecting the rest of the assignment.

The presentation and structure of an assignment can sometimes be helped by the addition of extra subtitles. If a section of prose is rather long, it is useful to divide it into two or three separate sections, each with its own title. The general grammar should also be checked. Particularly in a long assignment, it is relatively easy to start with verbs in one tense, and then to change to another tense later. This may or may not detract from the piece of work, but it is best to be aware of the possibility.

Using the computer

Computers have revolutionised the writing process. This is particularly so of the final stages of producing an assignment, where minor additions or deletions may be required. The use of computers has also enabled a distinction to be made between the initial process of writing, of putting ideas down quickly, and the second process of editing and 'polishing up' the work.

The main point to make about using computers is to keep a copy of the assignment as it grows and develops. As soon as the document is started on the computer, besides keeping it on the 'floppy' disk, a copy should be made on the computer hard disk. The latter copy should be updated as the work on the assignment continues. If necessary, and depending upon the availability of computers, the document should also be saved on a second 'floppy' disk, in case the first one is lost. The two disks can be kept in different places.

When the assignment is submitted it is a good idea to keep a paper copy as well as the copy on disk. It is also worthwhile considering putting a header and/or footer on the document and cross-referencing this with the disk.

PRACTICAL ADVICE

Use an abbreviated header or footer to identify yourself and your course on the assignment. This may look something like this:

J.Smith / BA(Market.) / Mod.6 / Essay 2

The essential details of your name and course, and of the assignment number, can be located on every page of the assignment. You can also list all the reference numbers of your assignments on the outside label of the computer disk. You will then have an easy cross-referencing system, by which you will be able to locate all disk versions of your assignments. Besides putting your own name and department on the disk label, it is worthwhile incorporating your name into the 'name' of the disk if the system allows you to, so that if lost, it can be returned to you.

Particularly with longer assignments it is a good idea to divide your work into separate named documents on the disk. If it is all saved as one document, then a number of potential problems can arise. As the number of pages gets longer, the word processing program may be continually repaginating the document, and it will result in considerable time delays, when it is impossible to work on the document. In addition, should there be an unfortunate accident and some or all of the document is lost, if all the work is in one document the loss will obviously be far worse than if it had been subdivided into separate documents.

A long document is also inconvenient when editing changes are made. If a paragraph is altered or deleted, this may affect the way in which text is distributed over a number of pages. This could then require the reprinting of either the entire document, or at least a major part of it.

The best strategy then with a longer assignment, is to decide in advance the sections or chapters which would most conveniently make separate documents on the disk. Each document will require a separate name on the disk. A certain amount of care is needed with page numbering when using a system like this. There is no problem with the first document as the page numbering will start at 1 and continue consecutively. The first page of the second document will then require formating in order to continue numbering from the last page of document one. This system is not difficult to operate, but care is needed if a small addition is made to one document. This may result in text spreading over to another page and then the page numbering of all subsequent documents will require altering.

Although care is needed in these respects, such a system is safer to use to minimise the risk of losing material, and also much easier because of the shorter print runs which are required for each document.

The process of reading and altering text for editing can be difficult to carry out on the computer screen. Only a small part of the page can be read on the screen at any one time and to check on what has been written earlier entails much use of the scroll bars. It is far easier to make amendments on the paper copy first. These changes or additions can be made in red ink for easy reference, and then systematically changed on the disk.

Thinking about your reader

In a sense, all writing should have a particular kind of reader in mind. In the case of academic writing, the most likely readers are tutors and external examiners. The kinds of assignments which we have been discussing in this book, are unlikely to be located in libraries, with the wider readership that implies. Admittedly, research reports can be revised and submitted as journal articles, but this is likely to entail rewriting in order to comply with the needs of the particular journal. Tutors and examiners are looking for certain qualities in an assignment, and it is worth reviewing certain general aspects during the editing process.

One of the most difficult issues when writing an assignment is to know just how much factual information to include. At each academic level in all subjects, that are certain concepts and ideas which it is taken for granted that we know and understand, so we think we need not elaborate upon them in an assignment or examination. The difficult point is being quite certain which areas to eliminate and which areas to discuss and to show that we understand.

PRACTICAL ADVICE

There are general principles to bear in mind when determining what to include or leave out:

- Try to use the assignment as an opportunity for you to demonstrate the knowledge, understanding and reasoning powers which you possess;
- Try to show a sophistication of understanding an argument which you feel is at least commensurate with the level at which you are studying, and try to exceed that level if you can;
- If you can remember being expected to explain a concept at an earlier stage of your academic career, then it is probably unlikely that a detailed explanation is required at a higher level;
- Assignments are always limited by a number of words: try to include as much higher-level analysis within the allotted space as possible.

A simple example from chemistry might illustrate the dilemma. At the beginning of a chemistry course most students learn how to light a Bunsen burner safely and to change the nature of the flame by altering the intake of air. In an account of a simple laboratory experiment at this level, the teacher might expect a mention to be made about the adjustment of the Bunsen burner flame. Clearly, this would not be required in the later years of school. It would be assumed that the student possessed that knowledge.

The problem for the student is knowing when they have reached a stage in their academic development that enables them to omit an explanation of certain concepts. Another example of the same problem is that students of different ages can be given the same essay title, but with the expectation that older students would produce a more sophisticated response. History essays are a good example of this issue. 'Discuss the events which led up the the independence of India' is an essay title which might well elicit different types of answer from students of different ages.

Ethical issues

Although you should have considered ethical issues throughout the assignment, it is worthwhile having a final thought about a few key matters. Anonymity of people and institutions is one of these. It is a good idea to make a final check that there are no obvious clues as to the identity of individuals or organisations. In addition, there should be a check that all extracts from other works are indicated as such.

Finally, there are two important aspects of academic writing which are worth checking, and these are references to other cultures, and references to the gender of individuals and groups. Both of these issues are partly ethical, in the sense that they entail an appreciation of 'fairness' and how to make reference to people in an objective way. In addition, however, they reflect wider sociological issues, so are probably better considered separately.

References to other cultures

When referring to people of different cultural origin, one of the difficulties is choosing the correct term to use. One of the terms most commonly used is 'ethnic minorities'. This is probably because in many academic contexts, particularly where research studies are concerned, a discussion may involve people who have migrated from one country and culture to another, where they find themselves to be in the minority. However, the term is only strictly accurate in some contexts. In Britain, for example, Indian and Pakistani migrants are a minority group in the country as a whole, but there may be some areas where they form a 'majority' group. Moreover, although they may be a minority in most institutions such as schools, there may be some schools in which they are a majority. It is probably better to use the term 'ethnic minority' only when there is an explanation of the context.

There is another difficulty with the use of general terms such as 'people from the Indian subcontinent', or 'West Indian'. The problem is that they encompass individuals who may belong to significant subgroups, and yet the importance of those smaller groups is masked by the larger term. The Indian subcontinent, for example, has a number of major cultural groups, which are very different from each other, and are perhaps only united by the fact that they occur on the same subcontinent.

Hindus and Muslims, for example, are both religious *and* cultural groups. People from both groups live together in India, often in close proximity, yet retain different cultures. To group them together to say 'ethnic minorities' in Britain, does not fairly describe their own important cultural identity.

It is important in assignments, therefore, to adopt terms which are as precise as possible when describing different religious or cultural groups. If the most significant determinant of the group identity is religion, rather than country of origin, then it is probably better to use a religious name when describing the group.

PRACTICAL ADVICE

When selecting a name to describe an ethnic or cultural group, it is best to ask yourself the question: 'What is the main factor which unites this group and gives them their unique character?' The answer to this question will probably help to determine the most appropriate name to use.

Besides checking through the assignment that appropriate terms have been used for cultural groups, it is also important to ensure that there are no broad generalisations about the characteristics of a particular group. It can be a great temptation to write that all British people have certain characteristics, or that all Americans typically behave in a certain manner. These kinds of generalisations are problematic on two counts. First, it seems highly unlikely that there would exist satisfactory evidence to claim that all members of a cultural or racial group have a particular behavioural characteristic. Second, any generalisation about a social group risks being unfair to individuals who do not possess that characteristic.

A different but important aspect of making reference to other societies is the danger of appearing not to value the culture of that society. Suppose, for example, that we are discussing a country which has an essentially agrarian society, with little industrial development. We may quite easily refer to such a country as 'an underdeveloped country'. The problem with this phrase is that it can carry a subtle implication that it is not only the industrial infrastructure of the country which is underdeveloped, but that also in some vague way, the inhabitants of the country, too, are underdeveloped. There could be a feeling that the term is being applied to the entire societal structure of the country.

When editing an assignment it is a good idea to be careful about the use of such terms which might carry a pejorative connotation, if read and interpreted in a certain way. To avoid this difficulty, it is best to be precise in the choice of phrase. For example, if one wishes to suggest that a country has little industrial infrastructure at the moment, there are a variety of ways of saying this, without the use of the general word 'underdeveloped'. Examples might be as follows:

> Manufacturing industry is beginning to develop in the country.
>
> A factory building programme is being developed.
>
> The country is developing from an agrarian to a partly industrialised economy.
>
> Industrial manufacture is now increasing.

It is better, therefore, to make descriptive statements which are as close to the 'facts' as possible, rather than evaluative judgements.

In many ways, the word 'developing' is much better than 'underdeveloped', because it gives a sense of society evolving continuously. In that sense as well, the word 'developing' can legitimately be applied to, say, European industrialised countries. All countries are, in many senses, developing.

It is also important to acknowledge that there are groups of people in the world who may be less well developed industrially, but who may be more sophisticated in other ways. For examples, groups such as the indigenous peoples of the Arctic, Australia or the Amazon, may not have developed large-scale industry, but they possess many qualities which are perhaps only just being recognised in other parts of the world. For example, their existence is in harmony with their environment and they tend to consume few of the natural resources of the area.

> *PRACTICAL ADVICE*
>
> Try to avoid evaluative terms such as 'developed' when you describe other cultures or countries. Think of the particular quality to which you are trying to refer, and then describe it as accurately as possible.

One final aspect of referring to other cultures is the possibility of overlooking the significant advances made in some countries. For example, it is easy to assume that mathematical and scientific knowledge originated and developed in Europe. In fact, mathematical knowledge made major advances in India, while the study of chemistry was significantly advanced in Arab countries and in China. The assumption that one's own culture is in some way more significant that other cultures can be termed ethnocentrism. This kind of attitude can sometimes appear implicitly in writing which, for example, stresses the discoveries of certain scientists, at the expense of the advances made in other countries.

It is not always easy to find the most appropriate words and phrases to refer to other countries and cultures, but the above principles should help. The best strategy is to try to avoid too many evaluative phrases, and to describe cultures as accurately and as objectively as possible.

References to gender

It may be helpful to review some general principles in relation to gender in academic writing and then to consider writing styles which may need some amendment. One of the main issues in relation to gender is the tendency to use the masculine personal pronoun 'he' for all situations, even if the person referred to is female. There are many arguments which are advanced for this being undesirable. On one level, one might argue that it is simply unfair not to represent people who make up half the number of human beings. Other arguments point to the potential effect of representing a male-oriented vision of the world. The general principle is, therefore, to find a writing style which eliminates as far as possible an unfair emphasis upon the male gender.

A subset of this general issue is the need to avoid implying that some roles in society are necessarily likely to be occupied by men. When referring to, say, researchers or professors, the impression may be given that they are likely to be men. One might regard this as a tendency to gender stereotype particular roles. It should be avoided on the general grounds of unfairness, but also because it tends to reinforce a male-dominated view of the world.

This is only a brief review of a complex issue, but at least it points us towards some specific guidance in relation to checking and editing prose. The first necessity is to develop stylistic strategies for avoiding the sole use of 'he'. The use of the personal pronoun can occur in sentences such as:

> A researcher who is developing a questionnaire may find it difficult to refine the questions, and he may decide, therefore, to use a pilot survey.

There is really no need to imply 'he' in this sentence. It is clear that the subject of the sentence is not a specific researcher. If that was the case, then it would be perfectly legitimate to use whichever gender pronoun was appropriate. Here, it is clear that the singular subject merely refers to 'researchers in general', and therefore it seems unfair to use solely the male pronoun. The sentence can easily be rewritten in a number of ways:

> Researchers who are developing a questionnaire may find it difficult to refine the questions, and they may decide, therefore, to use a pilot survey.
>
> or
>
> Researchers who are developing a questionnaire may find it difficult to refine the questions, and may decide, therefore, to use a pilot survey.

This revision clearly depends upon using the subject in the plural, with or without the use of 'they'. A singular subject can, however, easily be retained:

A researcher who is developing a questionnaire may find it difficult to refine the questions, and may decide, therefore, to use a pilot survey.

or

When a questionnaire is being developed it may be difficult to refine the questions, and a researcher may decide, therefore, to use a pilot survey.

or

When one is developing a questionnaire it may be difficult to refine the questions, and one may decide, therefore, to use a pilot survey.

Some of these alternatives are more formal than others, but they do demonstrate that it is possible to avoid the use of the male personal pronoun.

There are other solutions to this problem which have been advocated by some including:

- the sole use of the female personal pronoun
- the alternate use of male and female pronouns
- the use of male pronoun for some situations or roles, and female pronoun for others

If it is the intention to adopt a specific combination of male and female pronouns, then it is probably best to explain the rationale and the system used, at the beginning of the essay or assignment. In this way the reader will be less likely to be confused by the use of both 'he' and 'she'.

Besides the use of pronouns, it is also important to avoid gender stereotyping. This can easily happen with work roles, and one of the commonest examples is a reference to doctors as male and nurses as female. Such stereotyping can also manifest itself in the assumption that senior executives of companies will be male. The key argument here is that stereotyping can easily reflect and reinforce prevalent gender distributions in society. In most cases when referring to particular job roles, there is no need to make any assumption about the gender of the role holder.

It is important to be aware of equal opportunities issues throughout the writing of an assignment, but sometimes during the editing process inadvertent errors can be corrected.

Checking references

By the time an assignment has reached the editing stage, most people probably do not feel like checking every reference and quotation for complete accuracy. It would be tedious and time consuming. The best policy is to try to get them as accurate as possible initially. However, there is a certain amount of routine checking which does not take too long and may quickly reveal an error or two.

- Make a check to see that no quotations or references mentioned in the text are omitted from the bibliography;
- Check that all quotations have an author and date attached to them;
- Check that page numbers are stated wherever necessary (such as with all quotations);
- Check that the bibliography or list of references uses a standard system, and that all authors are listed in alphabetical order.

These checks can be made fairly quickly, and in a long piece of work you may decide to check only a sample of quotations. While doing a word search on a computer is not an infallible way of checking references it can be a useful additional check.

Tutors do look at quotations and at the referencing system fairly closely. It is a part of an assignment which is open to easy scrutiny, in the sense that it can be checked rapidly, and errors show themselves easily. Most tutors will probably have neither the time nor inclination to check the accuracy of every quotation, but in many cases they will know at least whether an extract has been used appropriately. They will probably know some of the books in the bibliography in passing, and others they will known in detail. They will probably have a good idea whether an extract is a suitable choice for the assignment and whether it has been used in the correct context. They may decide to look up one or two of the quotations, either to check them, or merely out of interest.

Tutors will, however, certainly be looking to check if page numbers are given for quotations, and if a uniform system of referencing has been used.

Linking sections

In some kinds of assignment it is a useful idea to employ a numbering system for different sections. This is frequently employed for reports of various kinds, where there is a systematic structure. It is less common for essays, where there is a tendency to avoid too much subdivision into sections. In some reports or portfolios a decimal system is employed. If we imagine an example of an assignment concerning the environment, then the decimal system might be used as follows:

1\. The pollution of the environment

1.1 Air pollution

1.1.1 Sulphur dioxide emissions
1.1.2 Carbon dioxide concentration
1.1.3 Lead in the atmosphere

1.2 Chemical waste
1.2.1 Disposal of radioactive waste
1.2.2 Chemical in refuse landfill

The decimal system offers a clear and logical method of numbering sections in a document. It is particularly helpful where it is necessary to refer to other sections of an assignment, since a precise reference can be given.

A few simple checks can be made, which help the reading of an assignment. If there is a Contents page, then it can be worth checking the page numbers of sections on that page with the actual page numbers in the text. Some paragraphs may be long, and the reading of an assignment may be helped by dividing paragraphs where necessary. Numbering of pages may need checking to ensure, for example, that it is continuous between chapters or major sections.

Do not confuse your reader

It is sometimes all too easy for a writer to think that what they have written is logical and makes perfect sense at a first reading. Even checking the prose may not reveal phrases or sentences which are obscure or difficult. One useful strategy is to listen to what has been written rather than simply rereading it.

> ### *PRACTICAL ADVICE*
>
> It helps when editing to read the assignment out loud to yourself. It is often much easier to spot errors, or passages which could be rewritten, than by simply reading silently. Try reading part of the assignment and tape recording your voice. When you play the tape back, you may find that you have an entirely different perspective on the assignment.
>
> Alternatively, you can ask a friend to read the assignment to you.

A style of writing which can be confusing to the reader is one which incorporates the use of simile and metaphor. Clearly, some types of writing, particularly poetry, make extensive use of these literary forms, but in academic writing they can be confusing. Consider the following example:

> The research had been going like a dream when I realised I had shot myself in the foot with the sampling strategy.

This sentence incorporates both simile and metaphor. In the case of the simile 'like a dream', the writer's meaning is simply not clear. It presumably implies that the research is going well, but we are not clear whether this means it is succeeding in all respects, or merely in some aspects. Research rarely proceeds satisfactorily in absolutely every respect, and therefore perhaps we should assume the latter. Then, if that is the case, we really require more details on those aspects which are going well, and those which are going less well.

There is the same problem with the metaphor 'shot myself in the foot'. We presume the research has realised that a serious mistake has been made with regard to sampling, but we do not know the nature of the error. Again, the difficulty with the metaphor is that it is not sufficiently precise for the needs of academic writing. Simile and metaphor are used extensively in literary forms where it is necessary to create a particular impression or atmosphere, but where it is unnecessary to be conceptually or factually precise. The above sentence would have been better written something as follows:

> The data collection for the research appeared to be progressing well, when it was realised that an error had been made in generating the random sample.

Another aspect of an assignment which may require editing is when the reader is referred forwards in the assignment to an entry in another section, or perhaps backwards to a previous section. There is no problem with this providing that the reference is correct. It is wise, therefore, to check statements such as the following:

> Further discussion of this topic is included in the next section.

It is best to have a look in the next section to make sure that the discussion is present.

The conclusion of an assignment is another area where there is sometimes a need to refer to another section. For example:

> The evidence presented in Section 6 suggested that there had been an increase in economic activity.

It is sensible to check Section 6 to make sure that this is what was suggested. This is particularly important if you have done any renumbering.

PRACTICAL ADVICE

Editing an essay or report may not *seem* to be a very rewarding activity until the day you spot a howler *before* it gets seen by your tutor! You will already have spent a great deal of time on your assignment, and done the best you feel you can do but that final check through will usually produce something to make the effort worthwhile.

You will, of course, be very familiar with the content of the assignment, especially if you have been working on it right up to the last minute. You may well, therefore, be feeling rather jaded about it. One way of helping to overcome this is to do something completely different, even if it is only for half an hour, before you start editing.

It will probably be difficult to concentrate for long on the editing process. This is because you are frequently looking for quite small errors, and also your familiarity with the text tends to make the rereading rather less than exciting. In the light of this, you may find it easier to carry out the editing process in small stages rather than trying to complete it all at once.

If you have included tables or charts it is also a good idea to check the numbering sequence and that they are in the correct place. If you have altered the text you need to make sure the tables or charts still match it.

Printing the final copy

When all the editing is complete, the next stage is to print off the assignment and to make a quick check that the printout is the same as the version on the screen. It is always best to use a laser printer, if possible. The definition is much better, particularly where diagrams or charts have been used.

For a variety of reasons, the paper copy may not always correspond exactly with the version which was on the screen. This applies particularly at the end and beginning of pages. Without rereading the entire assignment, it is worth flicking through the pages, and looking for any obvious errors in the printing. These will have to be amended on the disk if any are evident.

Having obtained a good laser-printed copy, it is wise to photocopy this, so that you have your own copy. In addition, last checks should be made to ensure that there is at least one electronic copy of the material – on the hard disk or on another floppy.

Binding and dissemination

Although assignments are, and should be, assessed in terms of content, it is satisfying to submit a piece of work that looks professionally produced. Binding is also important because it preserves the assignment, and keeps it in good condition throughout its travels within the assessment system. This is not unimportant, since assignments may have to be sent through the post to external examiners, or pass through many hands at a moderation event.

Different kinds of assignments require binding in a different way. A portfolio for example, which typically will contain a large quantity of evidence, is often best kept in a box file, lever-arch file, or simple ring binder if the material is not too bulky. The material will have been catalogued in some way, and there will usually be an overview of the portfolio which explains the rationale for including particular pieces of evidence. This overview is probably best kept separate from the evidence, and can be included in a plastic wallet within the box file.

A seminar paper may need to be photocopied by the tutor, and it is probably better not to staple the pages. It can be enclosed in a plastic wallet.

An essay or research paper will need more protective binding. A ring binder is unnecessarily bulky for this type of assignment, and a slimmer folder is much better. There are a variety of binders on the market now, which incorporate a fairly strong transparent cover with a mechanism for loose-leaf binding. They are excellent for essays and research reports.

The assignment is now ready to hand in! One final thought as you do so. Some institutions have a system of giving students receipts for work when it is handed in. The dated receipt is useful as evidence of submission, and so it is best to obtain one if it is available.

If your institution does not have such a system you could try making an entry in a diary and just asking whoever you hand the assignment to if they would initial a note that they have received it.

Summary

- Try to remember that a tutor is limited in the nature of the advice which can be offered.
- Before you commence editing the assignment, reread the submission instructions.
- Keep a computer copy, either on the hard disk or an another floppy.
- Use headers and footers to cross-reference the paper copy with the disk.
- Divide a long assignment into separate documents on the disk.
- Think carefully about the ways of referring to gender or to other cultures.
- Try to avoid stereotyping, ethnocentrism, and evaluative terms such as 'underdeveloped'.

FURTHER READING

The following books provide further advice on aspects of academic writing:

Anderson, J and Poole, M (1994) *Thesis and assignment writing*, Milton, Qld, John Wiley and Sons

Barnes, R (1995) *Successful study for degrees*, London, Routledge

Barrass, R (1984) *Study*, London, Chapman and Hall

Barrass, R (1995) *Students must write*, London, Routledge

Clanchy, J and Ballard, B (1992) *How to write essays*, Melbourne, Longman Cheshire

Dunleavy, P (1986) *Studying for a degree in the Humanities and Social Sciences*, London, Macmillan

Hector-Taylor, M and Bonsall, M (eds) (1994) *Successful study*, Sheffield, Hallamshire Press

Hennessy, B (1995) *How to write an essay*, Plymouth, How to Books

Howe, A (1986) *How to study*, London, Kogan Page

Morison, M (1990) *Psychology essays and practicals*, Harlow, Longman

Murphy, S and Smith, M A (1991) *Writing portfolios*, Ontario, Pippin

NEBSM, (1991) *Project preparation*, Oxford, Pergamon

Rudestam, K E and Newton, R R (1992) *Surviving your dissertation*, London, Sage

Van Emden, J and Easteal, J (1993) *Report Writing*, Cheltenham, Stanley Thornes, second edition

The following general reference works may be useful when writing assignments:

Bryson, B (1984) *The Penguin dictionary of troublesome words*, Harmondsworth, Penguin

Bryson, B (1994) *The Penguin dictionary for writers and editors*, Harmondsworth, Penguin

Bullock, A *et al* (eds) (1988) *The Fontana dictionary of modern thought*, London, Fontana Press, second edition

Bullock, A and Woodings R B (eds) (1992) *The Fontana dictionary of modern thinkers*, London, Fontana Press

Cohen, J M and Cohen, M J (1995) *The Penguin dictionary of twentieth century quotations*, London, Penguin, second edition

Gowers, E (1987) *The complete plain words*, Harmondsworth, Penguin

Green, J (1991) *New words: a dictionary of neologisms since 1960*, London, Bloomsbury

Manser, M H (ed.) (1990) *Chambers dictionary of synonyms and antonyms*, Edinburgh, Chambers

Market House Books (1993) *The Oxford dictionary of abbreviations*, Oxford, Oxford University Press

Modern Humanities Research Association (1991) *MHRA style book*, London, Modern Humanities Research Association, fourth edition (Although this is aimed at writers of dissertations it contains a lot of useful general advice and it is not an expensive book.)

Oxford dictionary for writers and editors, Oxford, Clarendon Press

Phythian, B A (1980) *Teach yourself English grammar*, London, Hodder & Stoughton

Phythian, B A (1993) *Teach yourself a concise dictionary of correct English*, London, Hodder & Stoughton

You will probably already have a good dictionary but specialist subject dictionaries are also very useful. Similarily a thesaurus can be invaluable for those times you can't think of the right word.

GLOSSARY

Action research An approach to research with a very practical purpose. Action research involves identifying an issue or problem in a practical situation such as at work or in a large organisation. A strategy is then devised to investigate the issue, and the research data used to alter or improve the situation. Action research does not presuppose any particular methodology.

Anecdote An account of a personal experience. Generally, anecdotes are distrusted in research reports because they introduce an element of subjectivity. The anecdote is very personal research data, and is difficult to substantiate. However, anecdotes are employed in autobiographical and oral history accounts, and have a place in qualitative research.

Assessment The process of forming a judgement whether a particular piece of work meets the required standard for a particular course of study.

Assessment criteria The yardsticks by which a particular piece of student work is judged. Assessment criteria should be clear and precise, and capable of being applied as impartially as possible. Criteria imply *standards* of work. A criterion for example, may be that an assignment should have a detailed bibliography of relevant works, presented in a consistent format.

Assessor The tutor who assesses a piece of work. An internal assessor is a tutor within a college or university who marks the work of college students. An external assessor is a tutor from another institution who is employed to see a sample of work, and to check assessment procedures and comparability of standards between institutions.

Causality The idea that a change in one variable is a direct consequence of a change in another variable. Causality is very difficult to demonstrate in absolute terms in any research. It is particularly difficult to show in research in the social sciences because of the large number of potential variables involved.

Bibliography A list of works which have been consulted during the preparation of an assignment. The works may include books, journal articles, pamphlets, newspaper articles, unpublished material and other sources. The works should be listed by alphabetical order of author surname, using a standard system such as the Harvard System.

Citation A reference to a work which has been consulted for an assignment.

Concept An idea which we hold about something. *Goodness* for example, is a concept. It means different things to different people. It is important in an assignment to define concepts clearly. If there is no general agreement about the use of a concept, then its significance in that particular assignment should be clarified.

Critical A word used in assignments to indicate *clear-thinking*, *analytic*, or *carefully-considered* processes. The word is not used in any sense to mean *criticise*. It is employed in phrases such as 'a critical discussion of a topic' or a 'critical account of an issue'.

Dissertation An account of a research investigation submitted as part requirement for a university degree. Most Masters degrees conclude with a dissertation, but the term is particularly used with research degrees such as the Master and Doctor of Philosophy. If the dissertation is accepted for the degree, then it is usually bound like a book, and a copy lodged in the university library. Students who submit a dissertation are usually asked to undertake an oral examination about the research, called a *viva voce* examination. The term *dissertation* is generally interchangeable with the term *thesis*.

Empirical A word usually used with *data* to signify evidence which is collected through experimentation or observation. Empirical data is research data which is collected using the powers of the senses such as sight or hearing. It is contrasted with data obtained by the analysis of concepts, as in philosophy.

Ethnography An approach to research which is derived historically from anthropology. An ethnographic investigation involves a detailed study of an organisation or a social group, and can involve interviews and participant observation. Ethnographers are particularly interested in the views and interpretations of the people who are the subject of the study.

Grading The aspect of assessment which involves the allocation of a percentage or grade to an assignment. A percentage is referred to as a 'numerical grade', whereas a letter is termed a 'literal' grade. If an assessment is regarded as 'ungraded' then the assignment is simply described as 'pass' or 'fail'.

Harvard System A system of referring to books or articles in an assignment. The author's surname and data of publication are cited in the text, and the full details of the work are listed in the bibliography or list of references at the end of the assignment.

Hypothesis An 'intelligent' guess about a possible relationship between variables. The development of a hypothesis is one of the first stages in a research investigation. The researcher then collects data to try to support or negate the hypothesis. A hypothesis is not 'proven' but may be provisionally 'supported'.

Interviewee A person who provides data during an interview.

Learning outcomes On many college and university courses modules of study are frequently expressed in terms of 'learning outcomes'. These are statements of what the student is expected to know when the module is completed. Learning outcomes may involve the acquisition of knowledge or understanding, or may be concerned with the learning of new skills or competences.

Methodology The area of study which includes all of the aspects of a research design. Methodology embraces the different techniques of data collection and of analysis, discussion of the justification for different research designs, the ethics of research, and the theoretical underpinnings of different research approaches. Research plans and reports usually contain a discussion of methodological issues.

Moderation The process whereby assessors (moderators) compare the quality and grading of pieces of work from different courses or institutions. The purpose of the exercise is to ensure comparability of standards between courses. Moderation can take place either within an institution, or between two different institutions.

Module A unit of study on an academic course. Modules can exist at different academic levels, for example at undergraduate or postgraduate levels, and they can be of different 'sizes' normally expressed as a number of credit points. A course can be modularised without necessarily being part of a credit accumulation system, but generally modules can be used to build up credit towards a particular academic award.

Natural sciences A term generally used to distinguish subjects such as physics, chemistry or geology, as opposed to the social sciences of sociology and psychology.

Objectivity A characteristic of an enquiry which does not rely upon the interpretation or understanding of a single individual. An objective enquiry looks at different perspectives and viewpoints, and concedes the possibility of multiple interpretation.

Paradigm An all-embracing world-view of concepts and ideas which provides an integrated framework within which the individual operates and interprets the world. An example would be to say that 'the argument has been constructed within a scientific paradigm'.

Perspective This term has much in common with 'paradigm'. However, it is usually employed in a rather more restricted sense. One might speak of operating within the perspective of a particular writer or thinker. 'Perspective' is also used to refer to the concepts, ideas and writings of particular thinkers. In sociology, for example, one speaks of a study of the main theoretical perspectives of the subject.

Plagiarism The use of the work of another person as if it were one's own. Plagiarism is avoided in academic writing by ensuring that where there is a direct quotation from another book, the source of the extract is given.

Portfolio A collection of artefacts or evidence. The term is typically used to refer to a collection of evidence which is submitted to meet the requirements either of entry to a course, or for academic credit on that programme.

Qualitative In research, usually used to refer to qualitative data, meaning data which consists of words rather than numbers. Qualitative data collection would typically involve interviews or observation studies. In the former case the evidence is in the form of the spoken words used in the interview, while in the latter case it employs the written accounts of the researcher or observer.

Quantitative A data collection method which involves using numerical data. It is normally associated with statistical analysis.

Random sample A sampling procedure in which each member of the total population has an equal chance of being selected for the sample. The traditional way of achieving this is 'to put names in a hat'. A more methodical way is to use random number tables which are devised for the purpose of sampling. Much statistical analysis is predicated upon the assumption of a random sample.

Reliability A data collection instrument is reliable if when it is used on two occasions, separated by a period of time, it yields consistent results.

Respondent The individual who provides data for the researcher during an investigation.

Scientific method The general approach whereby hypotheses are tested in a systematic manner. From a preliminary examination of a research issue or problem, the researcher generates one or more hypotheses, which purport to indicate the relationship between variables. A research design is then developed to examine these hypotheses. The latter are either provisionally supported or negated by the data. If supported, the hypotheses may be developed into a provisional theory. The latter then suggests new hypotheses for testing. If at any stage the hypotheses are negated, then the theory cannot stand in its present form and must be revised. The process is then repeated.

Seminar A meeting consisting usually of tutor and small group of students, convened to discuss a particular issue of academic interest. A seminar paper is often presented by a member of the group, in order to facilitate the discussion. The seminar paper, if presented by a student, may form the basis of an assessment on the particular course of study.

Theory A statement which explains the relationship between a number of variables. A good theory should have wide applicability to a number of contexts, and should also be capable of predicting future interactions between variables. Implicit in a theory is also the notion of the cause of events and the reasons for one variable being affected by another. These features are present to varying degrees in different theories. Theories can only be provisional. They can only be supported as long as there is no evidence to the contrary.

Thesis Another term for a dissertation.

Time management The extent to which one can structure working time effectively and efficiently. Time-management skills are particularly significant for students working on assignments and for researchers conducting investigations and preparing dissertations.

Tutorial A discussion (usually one-to-one) between tutor and student, in order to explore a particular academic issue.

Validity A data collection instrument is valid if it actually measures what it sets out to measure, e.g. an interview schedule designed to collect data about attitudes of respondents is only valid if the respondents are revealing their genuine attitudes.

INDEX